THE HOUSE & THE CLOUD

BUILDING A COMPELLING VALUE PROPOSITION USING RISK AWARENESS TO SELL TECHNOLOGY

DAVID STELZL

The House & the Cloud, *Building a Compelling Value Proposition Using Risk Awareness to Sell Technology*

For more information about this title or other books and/or electronic media, contact the publisher at: SVLC, PO Box 628 Waxhaw, NC 28173

Printed in the United States of America

Cover Design by David Stelzl

ISBN-9781505396621

“MAKING MONEY W/ SECURITY”

“Your stuff works Dave, Thanks for the advice! I like to deal with CEO’s only, in the SMB space, because they have the checkbook; they are the asset owners. Talking to them about technology is really tough. But when talking about Operational Efficiencies, Data Risk, or obtaining those efficiencies and Costs reductions, I can tell you my margins have doubled, sales are taken to a higher level, and the CIO/IT guy and the CFO are now only supporters or influencers, not decision makers. This has opened up a whole new sales discussion and approach.”

- Doug Baker, President ICE

“We recently held an educational event with David Stelzl as our keynote speaker to explain the 7 Essential Mindsets of securing critical data. The event was held at the right time, with the right people, and at the right place and was a great success! We had 74 people in attendance which represented 31 actual companies. Of those, 65% signed up for a Risk Assessment that night and an additional 5 companies wanted project work done. Since then, we’ve had two of 31 companies actually call us for help with security issues. Both have engaged for project work. They definitely would not have called without us doing the event.

Judging the success of the educational event alone, I would be thrilled But something very powerful happened afterwards that I did not expect. A “Security” specialty opens doors even when my competitors are standing in them. In two meetings last week, I was discussing critical data with business owners as a follow-up to the event. Those owners gave me access to the entire network, passwords, interviews with staff, and most importantly TIME with themselves. I never could have had quality appointments like that without first delivering quality and value to those owners through the educational event with David Stelzl. When time is money and every second counts, the meetings I choose to attend must be valuable. The security specialty and Stelzl's message has given me an open door to pinpoint the holes in security that businesses have and allows me a quality conversation to remedy those holes. The specialty eliminates the typical roadblocks from internal/external IT people protecting their domains—even at the risk of the business being insecure. The result: meetings that get to the REAL problem, proposals with a higher close rate, solutions that are custom designed and valuable to the owner. Now that is a win-win.."

- Nate Freedman, President Network People

I wanted to sincerely thank you for the impact you have had on my business (Earthwave) all the way out here in Sydney – Australia.

By simply following your strategy and adopting the House & the Cloud sales strategies I have been able to completely re-engineer my go-to-market approach that is actually ideal for any MSSP, as it brings home the importance of Detection & Response.

I have pushed these strategies to my channel partners as part of our channel program, and helped them align their strategies with ours. So by simply extending your Educational Marketing message, now I have more committed partners who are actively taking us in front of their customers knowing well the powerful messaging we are going to deliver.

I have witnessed average channel partner reps apply themselves to your model and have literally transformed themselves into great security sales people that are now highly sought after. In my opinion, any sales person could do the same if they just took the time to read and apply them selves.

Carlo Minassian, CEO Earthwave

TABLE OF CONTENTS

PREFACE

Information Security

The end of point product selling as you know it.

In the first edition of this book, back in 2007, back before the most recent recession, before cloud computing, BYOD (Bring Your Own Device) initiatives, the smartphone and the app craze, the social media explosion, and Google HangOuts,...and just about any of the really cool technology developments we have all come to love, I wrote, "Your elevator pitch is like throwing up on your client." A lot's changed since then, but this hasn't. Technology sales messaging is worse than ever. The products have continued to commoditize, and new innovations are racing through Geoffrey Moore's TALC (Technology Adoption Life Cycle) faster than ever (*See Moore's book describing the TALC – Insider the Tornado, 1995*).

Margin pressure is at it's all time high. The age of innovation has been replaced by inexpensive computing platforms that you can't possibly making a living selling – smartphones, tablets, and software we now call apps – downloadables priced at $.99. And while many of you are resisting the move to cloud, because it's not really a secure computing platform, it's happening. You can fight it. Business owners will continue to trade security for cost savings and flexibility every time. You won't win this one.

Every reseller, yours and those you compete with, now has

some form of managed services. They're all competing on price to win the most recurring revenue contracts at the lowest bid. Something's wrong with this. How low can you possibly go and still make a profit?

Meanwhile, the security problem is growing faster than anyone might have imagined. In the year 2000, my manager at Dimension Data (the last technology company I worked directly for) asked me if I thought security would still be a strong focus area in the new millennium. He didn't think so. Since then we've gone from small viruses to major botnets, espionage, nation state sponsored attacks, government infiltration, and security experts telling us that, "Every major company in America has been compromised by hackers." Does it sound like there's an opportunity to you? At the same time, you and your competition are likely competing on price, because every technology seems to be a commodity. I meet sales people everyday who are being pressed harder and harder to get the job done. Regardless of commoditization, they're pressed to sell more to make up for sinking gross profit margins. Their reward is a smaller paycheck.

I'm rewriting this book to stop the chaos. To guide you back to reality, and to point you in the direction of opportunity and profitability. There's still a profit to be made because there's still a major need!

Every company out there needs security right now! And as I've stated in hundreds of *Making Money w/ Security* Workshops, "Security is not a product, it's a discipline, and therefore it doesn't commoditize." Commodity is more of a mindset than anything. It's how you sell it, not what it is.

Let me begin with the radical idea that just about everything you see others doing in the channel is wrong. Most of the marketing dollars and ideology today is coming through manufacturing channel management. However most of the channel marketing people out there have no experience actually selling or marketing on the reseller side. I know they mean well, but until you've tried to run a profitable reseller business, it's hard to really know what does work and what doesn't. As a result, billions of dollars and countless leads are wasted every year. I'm talking about money that could be used to drive real business opportunities for your company, if only you had a system that predictably worked.

Vendors are used to brand-building and selling with a recognized brand. Having coached direct sales teams all over the world, I know it's true. On the other hand, all resellers sell the same brand. There is no competitive advantage on the product side of their business. And they can't look to the vendor for any real competitive advantage.

They can't look at other resellers either. Most of the new deals come from referrals. That would be okay, except for the fact that there aren't enough of these referral leads to go around. Security sales have been driven my compliance and intrusions for the most part, however this too makes for a tough sales process. Compliance has become more political than anything else, making for long drawn out sales cycles. Most companies who actually experience a security intrusion problem don't know it, and therefore are not going to call you. And about 80% of the purchasing decisions being made by your prospects are made by IT people searching Google, long before they ever contact you for a quote.

The fact is that most of your peers are blind to the real opportunity and will continue to pitch products at bigger discounts, and will continue to deliver less value, taking home smaller paychecks. Eventually these product sales will be done by inside sales people making half of what you're accustomed to. Don't follow them. The proof is in the metrics. Conversion numbers are the only thing you can really trust.

Consider The Wall Street Journal (WSJ). They've been writing almost daily for ten years on security issues. Other technology subjects come and go, but this one remains. Right now the big topics are Big Data, Cloud, and Mobility. They're attracting readers, so the WSJ is writing about them. But security is still in there and will continue to be, long after Big Data is on the shelf with data warehousing and voice over IP (VoIP.) And managed services is hardly anything worth talking about – the boom is over. The point is, the WSJ is looking for the same thing you are, conversion. They want people who don't read their news reports to start reading them, and keep reading. They want subscribers. And with all of the free news out there, they have a tough road ahead of them. They're counting on security, and the latest high-tech trends to keep CIOs interested in the CIO Journal (a section of the WSJ dedicated to IT leadership) – a $500/year habit they hope will continue.

In the year 2000, people would attend a lunch & learn meeting to learn about voice over IP (VoIP). Hold that same meeting today and you'll be lucky to get a few bored IT people looking for a free lunch. On the other hand, I've held dozens of lunch & learns with a security focus over the past several years. Our audiences range from with 30 to 50 people – all executives. Our conversion rates range from 70% - 90%, with a handful at a full 100% conversion. I'm talking about people who can buy, signing up on the spot for a security assessment. There are other topics that come and go with strong results, but they're not product pitches on storage, servers, VoIP, or data center. And they're not coming to hear about managed services either.

Crossing the Great Divide

Next, I offer the even more radical and challenging idea that pretty much everything you've been led to believe by the manufacturers as, "Guaranteed to Succeed," is wrong. I'm speaking mainly to the reseller here simply because 90% of the sales are going to be channel sales in the coming years. So the message applies even if you sit on the vendor side of the fence.

Here's the great divide. On one side you have the resellers who are living on certifications and partner status. These companies are trying to build a business on their reputation as the go-to provider for a certain box brand. They're hoping for leads and bluebird deals. This works for one reseller in a given market, in a given city. Usually its the company that sells the most product for that manufacturer, regardless of their expertise or value to the customer. If that's not you, you're not going to win using this strategy. Their marketing programs will be all about products and features, not customer benefits. And their brochureware will be feature-function data sheets with zero sales conversion. This is not selling, it's order taking.

On the other side you have sales people who are making the move from Vendor to Advisor. But not just in name – in approach. These people are watching the trends, seeing what companies really need, and becoming experts in helping these companies deal with real business problems. The most predictable problem of all is that of poor security.

If you get this, you'll want to smack yourself for not seeing it sooner. It's not about the product, it's about the data. These companies are using data to make money, and when it's not there, not secure, not available, or not right, the business doesn't work. Once you see it, you'll never walk out of a sales meeting again thinking there's no opportunity. Every company has a security problem – the question is, will they see it, and if so, who will they look to (and pay) to solve it? From there you'll begin making changes to the way you sell, the way you approach new companies, who you meet with, and where you begin your sales questioning process. Your marketing will completely change, along with your prospecting, your marketing events, and the elevator pitch you recite in your head before each meeting.

Suddenly, most of the people around you will sound irrelevant, and they will be.

The astounding results you'll see from conversion numbers will convince you. When you see more than half of the group at a completely reengineered, security focused, lunch & learn, you'll have the courage and discipline to stay the course. Others might think you're narrow minded or that you're giving up opportunity by being so tightly focused, but I assure you, your numbers will make their opinions meaningless. And the value you are bringing to your clients will be so much more rewarding. Suddenly you'll be thinking, technology sales is an exciting place to be.

Over the past five years I have traveled around the world many times with this message. I've been to Australia, Singapore, India, Central America, Caribbean Islands, and South Africa with this message. The world's leading manufacturers of technology have spent a lot of time and money to get this message to their direct sales, channel sales, federal sales, and their largest reseller partners for one reason…it works.

Don't be fooled here! This is not a book about security! It's a marketing book. The House & the Cloud is a marketing message – a powerful message of hope. What is marketing? It's getting the right message in front of the right person, at the right time – and it goes hand in hand with sales. But it has to be compelling; it must be urgent. And no message is more urgent right now in the life of technology users (those making money with technology) than security. This book is not about using better technology or even improving your marketing. It is about totally transforming your approach and using a completely different kind of message. A message that is so urgent, if people don't listen, they might just be out of business. With that kind of message, you have to feel good about calling on the highest levels of the market you serve.

In this book I'll give you the rules. You might find them too strict. I'm not forcing you here to copy everything I say, but I am giving you a very straightforward message that is specific and effective. But I will also give you the principles behind the message. I'll explain exactly why it works so that as you become comfortable with it, you'll be able to modify it in ways that make it your message. As long as you stick to the underlying principles, you'll be able to craft all kinds of messaging that works.

Here's the basic roadmap of the journey your about to take:

- ☐ **Security Is Urgent and Everyone Needs It**. Despite what IT (Information Technology) people are saying, no company out there has it covered. To start, I'll give you some high level background on where we've come from and what's happening now in the security space. I'll also provide proof that every company out there has an urgent problem – that in most cases is not being adequately addressed.

- ☐ **The Message That Has Converted Countless Executives in Just 60 Minutes**. On average 75% of every executive audience I speak to converts immediately to an assessment. I'll show you exactly what I say and why they convert. Do what I'm telling you and you're guaranteed three meetings with an executive. If you still can't convert, there's a bigger sales problem that needs to be addressed.

- ☐ **Creating Undeniable Justification**. In the last part of the book I review the assessment process – a process that many of my clients are using to convert their clients to projects and managed services with a 90% success rate. It's simple, straightforward, and completely different from what I see most companies doing.

An Incredible Opportunity – Join the SVLC Insider's Circle!

Who else wants to be in the single best business – one of working with business leaders, knowing you're a critical part of their success?

You won't find over-promises, untested ideas, idle boasting, or get rich quick schemes here. The SVLC Insider's Circle is the real deal. It's a program that will transform your business. If you've ever followed sports you know that personal trainers and coaches are a key part of the player's success. The Insider's Circle is just that – a coaching program created for technology sales and marketing professionals just like you. It includes practical, doable steps, tools, live online training and Q&A sessions, and proven strategies to help you harness the powers of marketing, sales strategy, and technology to transform your business. You'll find:

- ☐ Live training sessions on gaining access to decision makers, advising them, and demonstrating unique value to them.
- ☐ The latest in technology trends and where to focus your efforts and professional development.
- ☐ A place to get help with your sales and marketing efforts through collaboration and Q&A.
- ☐ Recorded videos on how to use the House & the Cloud to gain access to the highest levels of the companies you serve.
- ☐ Mastery Programs on topics that will dramatically improve your sales and consulting process.

Join us today and begin making the move from selling point products to truly advising business level clients on the best uses of technology – make the move from Vendor to Advisor:

Visit us online at www.stelzl.us > business-strategies – and Test Drive the Insider's Circle.

CHAPTER ONE

Why Sell Security?

More than ever – every company you call on has a security need. Security has the power to differentiate commodity products, increase gross margin, accelerate sales cycles, and open new doors that might not be opened any other say.

Remember the mid-nineties? Reseller hardware margins were in the 30s and 40s. Software had even more margin. And bill rates were in the $120 – $175 range! Whether you work for a high-tech manufacturer selling your own brand of technology products, or you own or manage a solution-provider company that resells computers and networking equipment, you're keenly aware of what's happened over the last two decades.

Every manufacturer in the high-tech industry is fighting to maintain street price while working hard to hold their profit margins. Channel managers are working to get greater mindshare from their resellers. They are urgently working to help them find incremental business. Meanwhile, resellers are trying everything from bundling products and services, creating managed services offerings, to eliminating products altogether to grow the bottom line.

Over the last decade I've spoken with thousands of high-tech salespeople, sales managers, and owners of reseller businesses, each of whom shares a similar story. Many started technology companies 20 or more years ago, hoping to build a brand that would provide high earnings as computer usage and complexity skyrocketed in the nineties. Many had technical backgrounds with a vision to create something exciting that would yield riches beyond any technical or presales consultant salary. I often hear people talking about early retirement. But something's changed. I don't hear these things anymore.

Technology Companies, Boom to Bust

I met Norm at a Venture Tech Network Conference back in 2004. I had just finished delivering a session on reseller business strategies. Over a hundred reseller business owners were in my session that morning. For one hour I recalled the truths presented by Geoffrey Moore in his book *Inside the Tornado,* applying them to the reseller market. I was showing these business leaders how to recover from the Y2K implosion.

Just a few years earlier these resellers had been growing with no end in sight. In fact, I had been a part of a start up back in1995, that began as a small offshoot of an eight million dollar CAD-CAM business. Almost over night we turned this small company into a seventy-five million dollar integration company selling everything from storage and servers to networks and security. Most of these business owners, including Norm, had had dreams of retiring early. VARs (Value-Added Resellers) were selling for multiples of their revenue,. But the year 2000 changed everything.

If you were around during that time, you know that VAR business valuations went down to nearly nothing. Before we knew it the booming stock prices of just about every high-tech company were down to single digits. Cisco's market cap went from a whopping $555.5 billion down to 151 billion in just a few short months. Many resellers were on their way out of business, and Norm's company was one of them.

Every Business Owner's Dream

In my session I had explained the cycles of product commoditization and the need to build a more programmatic approach to reaching the market. I showed this group how to use consultative assessments to quickly convert to meaningful project work. A strategy that would eventually transition into long-term managed services contracts. At the end of my session a line of VAR business owners stood before me, hoping to sign up for a short 30 minute business review that afternoon – Norm was first in line.

His dream was to get his company, Computer Corner, back on track, and hopefully retire so he could spend more time with his growing family of grandchildren. Standing next to Norm was a young man named Randy, who I soon learned was actually his son. Randy had started working with him right out of high school doing odd jobs, cutting grass, keeping up the office, etc. Eventually he had transitioned to a field engineering role, working with PCs.

Standing in front of me, Norm had some big dreams in mind. Just months earlier their company had been nearly out of business. It was during that time that Randy came up with the brilliant idea of selling block hours for support. Things were starting to look up, but they needed a lot more before they could consider Norm's exit strategy. Norm was looking for some answers. How could he transition his company to a more profitable model like the one I had described in my session? (Note: You can find a detailed explanation of this transition process in my book, *From Vendor to Adviser*.)

It was during our 30 minute session that our plan came together. Norm asked me if I could work with Randy, enrolling him in my Mastery Group Coaching Program. We agreed to get started as soon as we returned from the conference.

The Surprising Power of Security

My first recommendation was to change the company name to something that sounded more consultative. That day, Sklar Technology Partners was born. My second recommendation was to focus on something with high-growth potential. **One of the first principles of marketing is, "Intense focus creates divergence**."

"It was hard to make the transition," Randy recalled in a recent interview. "The temptation is to be everything to everyone. After all, you don't want to turn down any business, especially when business is down."

But security is a powerful tool when it comes to marketing and attracting new clients. Every business needs better security. It wasn't long before the fruit of these changes became apparent in Randy's business. Using live lunch & learns, I worked with Randy to develop executive level invitations, call scripts, and most importantly, a conversion plan. (The details of this entire strategy are provided in a comprehensive step-by-step program I call *The Event Marketing Success Kit – Seven Secrets to Profitability Using Lunch & Learns and Sales Events* – available on my web store at www.stelzl.us)

Conversion Is the Only Thing That Matters

The first lesson for the newly branded Sklar Technology Team was "conversion". Past lunch & learns had been focused on what VARs refer to as, "Butts in Seats." In the new paradigm, the number of attendees doesn't really matter. It's conversion we're after.

The plan was pretty straight forward. We were going after the SMB (Small Medium Business) market, inviting business owners to an exclusive event. It could have been any market, but by tightly defining it, Sklar was able to position themselves as an expert in that specific market.

The invitations and call scripts highlighted growing concerns of information security risks and the need for business owners to get involved. My job, as an author/consultant was to share global trends and explore the major issues small businesses are running into due to their misunderstanding of cybercrime. In our session we offered a straightforward complementary assessment that would be used to help them determine their actual risk. If their company was in good shape, there would be no need to take action, just a recommendation to be constantly checking. If we did find something urgent, we would give them a prescriptive plan to get well.

Our first event was held at the local Richmond Sheraton. We had about 30 business owners present that day. It was a great showing for Randy's first executive event. I recall how excited Norm and Randy were as they set out their logo mugs, mouse mats, and data sheets. But the focus of this meeting was "conversion." At the end of our two hour meeting, over 90% of these business owners were signed up for the Sklar assessment.

It was complementary, but that was the plan. Our goal was conversion, not profit. Marketing is a process of attracting highly qualified buyers, giving them the right message, and leading them to the appropriate action. In this case, we had compelling justification that everyone in that room should sign up. Only a couple of people didn't see the need (In the *Marketing Success Kit* I explain how to follow up with those who don't see the need, as well as those who don't attend).

Great Assessments Bring Great Profits

It was a simple win-win strategy. We knew that these business owners had significant investments in their companies. A major data breach could land them in a lawsuit or even bankruptcy court. We also knew that their security strategies were probably non-existent. My keynote that day was a simple, story-filled program, to show them the major current threats, the mistakes most businesses were making at the time, and the need to assess on a regular basis in order to avoid big trouble. They saw it and acted on it by signing up. The profits came in two forms. Dollars and value. While we most often view dollars as the only profit that matters, gaining a life long customer and referral source is worth an incredible amount of money. The value of this type of approach far exceeds any product sale.

The assessment process was next. It was complementary to ensure a high conversion rate from the attendees. Those who made an effort to actually drive to this event, and then sign up, presented a highly qualified group of candidates. This is the second major principle of marketing. **It does absolutely no good to set up a marketing process that attracts anyone and everyone. Instead, we need hurdles that parse the larger audience, selecting those who are really interested in getting something done.** Our event proved to be the perfect strategy to get Norm's company back on the road to profit.

Using a simple formula I had been developing for over a decade, we set out to conduct what I now refer to as an, "Asset Focused Assessment." We'll explore this in some detail in the later chapters of this book. For an in-depth look at how to sell and conduct an assessment like this, see my *Security Sales Mastery*

Program, details are in the last section of this book).

The results were clear. Over 90% of these assessments converted to remediation business. It was during this time that Randy was transitioning to a more significant leadership role. Through our weekly meetings he was learning the ropes of sales and marketing, and gaining the wisdom he needed to grow this company. Over the next year Randy would come to master the process of conducting assessments and presenting the results to close business. In every single case we found major security holes that needed to be filled, and in most cases we were able to persuade business owners to take action.

Building Financial Stability For Long Term Success

At this point I explained to Randy the need for financial stability. Most VARs are living from product sale to product sale, and in some cases from project to project. Just the instability of the services model and utilization numbers will crush a small reseller. With this in mind, our next step was to develop a managed program that would create long term stability and profitability for his company. Every business should have a recurring revenue model or continuity program built into the overall solution strategy. Another way of saying this is, all sales should lead to recurring revenue to build financial stability. I would frequently tell Randy, "At some point you won't even want customers that aren't interested in your managed services program."

Again, we used security as our starting point. Using some of the early managed services tools just coming to market, we began to build a managed services offering. In each case we used the security value proposition to drive new business. Prospecting would begin with hosting the event, leveraging the assessment, fixing the issues through professional services offerings, and then moving the client into a managed program.

Basically the process went like this:

- ☐ Attraction – Getting qualified business owners to attend an informative luncheon meeting.
- ☐ Education – Showing them their need, at a business level.
- ☐ Assessment – Discovering their risks through a series of onsite meetings.
- ☐ Remediation – Addressing their urgent issues through project services.
- ☐ Managed Services – Maintaining an acceptable level of risk through an ongoing continuity program.

While many companies have attempted to do this, the downfall has been in the lack of focus on something that consistently moves people to action; and more importantly, a process that consistently converts a high percentage of those being marketed to. For Randy, security was the magnet. And the powerful combination of our event strategy and assessment process yielded a significant conversion rate to fee-based business. As long as the people coming to the events were well qualified, the investments being made in the complementary assessment were well justified. Make no mistake, these complementary assessments were not free. They had to be qualified, and the client's time investment was real.

Randy's Business Passed the Test

The test is profitable growth over time. Today Randy starts every month with a profit. Incremental sales bring greater profitability. But even if nothing gets sold, the company is still profitable because the business is built on the secure platform of annuity business. Now that doesn't mean he doesn't have to sell anything. All annuity businesses are constantly adding people if they are successful. Meanwhile, no matter how good you are, people are going to leave the program. In this business, you're either growing or shrinking. The key is to add more than you lose.

Looking back over the past decade, Randy's company has stood the test of time. The economy has been up and down. As I write this book, things are okay out there, but my financially savvy friends and family members tell me not to be too free with spending. If business is growing, it's important to be growing the right business. The future is unpredictable. A solid base of annuity customers is critical to long term financial stability.

Growing your customer base is also important. That requires a message that will cut through a crowded marketplace and provide justification that will move people in your direction as quickly as possible.

In order to do this, your company needs three things:

- ☐ A message of differentiation – not commodity products.
- ☐ A method to reach people at the right level.
- ☐ A process of consistent conversion.

Winning the War

So, how do technology companies fight against the forces of commoditization? And how does security create greater margins and offer greater business stability? How does it aid in the conversion process?

Whether you're selling on the frontlines, running a sales organization, own part or all of a reseller company, or work on the channel side, you need to understand security's strategic value and how to use its growing momentum to drive high-tech sales.

VARs Are Being Pushed In Too Many Directions

It's no surprise that technology resellers are struggling with margins, but is security really a solution?

Over the last fifteen years, the technology industry as a whole has dramatically changed. It's gone from a fast-growing, highly profitable business to one of thin margins. Over the past decade this has led to an increased interest in figuring out managed services.

In contrast, manufacturers of big boxes are pushing their resellers to focus on storage, data center, and hosted services (which are managed services.) The problem is, only the very largest of the big box resellers can really make a long term play with data center size projects. Hosted managed services can be provided by just about anyone with a partnership and a sales team. It's not unique. Today, a three person company can sell the same hosted solution sold by a 5oo Million Dollar Firm. Somewhere there needs to be a differentiator.

In Geoffrey Moore's Book, *Inside the Tornado*, he explains that the technology cycles come in waves of five to eight years. If you focus on one technology too heavily, chances are that technology will be commoditized and nearly worthless in just a few years. This is the fate of the average IP Telephony reseller right now. If you don't think so, just watch as sales decline and margins erode. Even if your profits manage to remain another two years, then what. Can you retool overnight?

CHAPTER TWO

The Power of Security

> Security is magnetic! However, security is not a product. All products eventually commoditize. By changing the way you view security, you'll see there is an amazingly powerful value proposition here that has the power to open almost any door.

The Average Security Sale Is A Commodity Sale Too

Security is always in the news, and generally ranked high on the company initiatives list. Is this a good place to put more focus? Most of the sales reps I know have been selling security appliances, but avoid higher-end security sales—a truism for both the manufacturer and reseller. Gross profits tend to be incremental and relatively low. Something obviously isn't working.

If you sell security appliances, you've likely noticed stiff competition can delay a sale by months. You may be able to take your family out for a fast-food meal with your commission check as margins shrink. You're frequently asked to place an evaluation product onsite, using free installation services to get it up and running. Either way, the manufacturer claims the product installs "in minutes," so there really isn't much consulting business for this product anyway. This hurts both the manufacturer and the reseller. You conclude this may not be the right place to focus.

Perhaps you've been in a meeting and the security topic came up. Excited, you recommend a follow-up meeting with your security expert. In turn, he agrees to bring his expert, and the resulting meeting turns into a feature/function battle. Again, you conclude this isn't worth the effort, so you return to commodity product sales.

Throughout the course of this book I hope to change this cycle. Each of these issues is symptomatic of treating security as a point product. By the end of this book you'll understand why every client has a security need—and by fulfilling this need you can produce significant profits. And it won't matter which technology niche or market you're calling on. In my opinion, when security is approached correctly it becomes highly profitable. It is a powerful door opener and something that is definitely not a commodity sale.

While working with a Chicago based company, I ran into Steve, an alumnus from one of my workshops. As I approached him, I could tell he was happy to see me. His words tell the tale: "I just turned an 80K opportunity into an 800K sale using the principles you taught us in your security workshop!" These are the same principles I'll share in the chapters to come.

It's not hard to sell security, but it does require a different approach—one you may not be used to taking. In the end, this book will give you a winning strategy for selling virtually any product or service by tying it to security. First, let's take a look at the value you bring to your clients.

An Incredible Value Proposition

What's your value proposition? How many times have you been asked, "What does your company do?" It's a simple question. But the answer may prove more complex than you imagine. Consider the following scenario:

You're attending an association meeting, social gathering, or group event. You meet someone new—perhaps an executive with a large manufacturing company in town. After striking up a conversation, an event organizer indicates he's ready to begin the meeting, and everyone is asked to be seated. Your new acquaintance quickly asks what your company does. You have only one minute before heading to your seat. What do you tell him?

Take a moment to write your answer on a sheet of paper. Underneath your answer, write a second sentence that explains the value your organization brings to prospective clients like the one you hypothetically met.

Every day you meet people. You're making phone calls, attending meetings, present at gatherings, or involved in some form of prospecting. But how many of these interactions actually turn into long-term profitable relationships? How often do you have a value proposition that resonates so strongly that your prospect wants to formally meet with you or schedule subsequent meetings? If you're a manufacturer with significant market share, you may have this value. For resellers, it's a different story.

As a reseller, brand is associated with your product offerings. Perhaps you sell Dell, HP, Cisco or some other globally recognized technology. But in the eyes of a CIO, there are thousands of companies just like yours. When this happens, price becomes your differentiation—and it will eventually destroy your company if your business model was built like those of most resellers: high-touch salespeople supported by highly trained presales engineers or consultants. It's an expensive model to run, unless you have a way to leverage all of that high-touch talent to close complex, margin-rich deals.

On the manufacturer's side, new companies appear every day

looking to steal your hard-earned market share. The commoditization of your products cuts into profits and destroys your channel. Future success depends on maintaining a leadership position and strengthening your channel.

Selling commodity products does not offer a compelling differentiation story, unless it's based on price and delivery—much the same way wholesale distribution is modeled. Consider the trends in nontechnical industries like supermarkets, hotel chains and bookstores. These industries are investing in customer experience and retention. In fact Forrester Research is telling us that software related to customer experience will be the high growth area in the coming years. Customers no longer want to shop in a basic grocery store. Instead, they demand cafés, prepared foods, banking services and a florist. Some stores will even shop for you.

Security has the power to transform your company's offerings if approached correctly. When leveraged correctly, it can create a value proposition that will completely transform business as you know it.

A Strategic Offering

Security may be the most strategic area to invest in right now. In my experience, security leads the list of what buyers need. But in this case, let's not call it security, let's call it Risk Mitigation.

The Only 4 Things Buyers Buy:

- ☐ Risk mitigation
- ☐ Operational Efficiency
- ☐ Competitive Advantage
- ☐ ROI (Return On Investment)

Of the four things buyers buy (which I cover in detail in my book, *From Vendor to Adviser*), security ranks first because fear of loss is our most powerful motivator. It is also extremely difficult to demonstrate the other priorities with basic technology infrastructure products. The second best one on the list is probably operational efficiency. If you can show a company eminent danger and you can show it to someone with true liability in a compelling way, chances are they'll take action. If you show them how to do something with greater efficiency and cost reduction, they'll probably buy it, but not if there's an emergency going on – like a cyber attack. Most security sales efforts fail to communicate true justification, but in the coming chapters I'll give you a proven strategy to accomplish this.

In my book, *From Vendor to Adviser* I go into some detail on all four, providing examples of how each would be approached. Still, security is number one. The point is, it doesn't matter what products or services your firm offers, when they are not sold in the context of one of these four things, price becomes the determining factor, and it is this focus on price that erodes margin.

A Fascination With Security

Here's an interesting way of looking at security. Do you read the WSJ (Wall Street Journal)-CIO Section? If you look at the articles written over the past two years you'll find many articles covering large manufacturers. It's generally Apple, Google, and small start-ups or IPOs like Twitter or Facebook that dominate these headlines. Other companies such as HP and Cisco will often show up whenever something important happens that might affect stock price.

The other headlines, and from my perspective, more interesting articles, have focused on Big Data, Cloud, Mobility, and Social Business or Social Media. But security is the long standing topic of choice. Looking back over ten years, only one has been in the news all along. Security.

It's important to note who the journalist's are writing to. IT does not read The WSJ. Business owners and business leaders are their customers. Clearly business leaders have a strong interest in security technology, trends, and events. In fact, it probably goes beyond just the CIO and CISO if they publish this to every subscriber of the Wall Street Journal. Given the importance here, security makes for a great topic of discussion when addressing any leadership team, as long as you do it at "The Wall Street Journal level."

The truth is, people are fascinated with security and cybercrime. If you hold a conference on data center or storage, IT people might attend. They're not decision makers. They are technology custodians looking for more education and perhaps a free meal. Advertise security trends, and if done right, you'll attract a much more qualified audience. When I work with resellers, I urge them to hold security seminars often. From the security platform, they can then go on to sell just about anything. Security has magnetic power to attract the right audience.

I recently coached a technology solutions company in the Midwest, (Let's call it ITS.) I worked with the president and a local marketing firm to mail personal letters to community business leaders. The letter described growing trends in information theft, current and future threats companies face, and the inadequacy of most corporate security strategies.

We planned a lunchtime event at a local restaurant, and I coached ITS' sales staff on how to convert attendees into clients incorporating the principles outlined in this book.

At the end of my presentation, I invited participants to a complimentary assessment from ITS. Fifty executives signed up to attend, 37 actually showed up, and 27 agreed to our assessment. The combination of a compelling topic and a well-executed plan gave the ITS team more opportunities than a cold-calling campaign would have delivered over several months—even more impressive because the executives involved were decision makers. Consider going through my *Event Marketing Success Kit* where I detail every aspect of conducting this type of meeting (www.stelzl.us > store.)

Everyone Needs Security

If I could show your clients how insecure their data really is—and the devastating impact of theft or misuse—I'd have a selling opportunity. Every company you're calling on could be in big trouble in the coming months if management fails to take action against looming threats. The FBI statistics show that the average malware lies dormant for about 250 days before being used against the company it has infected. But the average time to detect an actual attack is more like 14 months. So when a company says, "We've got it covered," or "There's no evidence of an attack here," it's a meaningless statement of ignorant confidence.

If we can identify a company's key assets and show some level of likelihood that they will suffer an attack, you have a sales opportunity. The secret to success is knowing how to message this back to the client at the leadership level.

The sophistication of today's threats and the perpetrators of cyber-crimes change daily, making most organizations more vulnerable than company leaders think. The "bad guys" are winning, and the consequences range from personal liability to business failure.

Better Business Bureau studies have cited identity theft as the fastest-growing crime in America, and child pornography as the fastest-growing Internet business. More than 200 million Americans' identity records have been exposed this year alone, and the number is growing all the time. In the JP Morgan breach of

2014 over two-thirds of U.S. households were impacted. Security experts tell us that just about everyone with a credit card has probably been compromised, the questions is, "When will my data be used fraudulently and will I discover it before something bad happens?"

While fear of losing information has not been sufficient to motivate executives to take action, justification of the extremely high likelihood of unauthorized access can. In reality, this is more than a standalone project; it's an infrastructure opportunity that can be enhanced and accelerated by using the security sales strategies covered in this book.

To begin this process, it's important to understand cyber-crime trends, who is behind them, and what they're doing to get in. Most companies assume they have acceptable security in place. In the chapters ahead, I'll cover who to talk to, what to talk about, how to create the necessary justification to convince them otherwise. In effect, security can do several things for you as you approach the sale. In the remaining pages of this chapter, let's take a look at what security does for you as the seller.

Board Level Access

In just about every sales workshop I've conducted, I ask the sales people if they've met with the board members for the companies they call on. In every session there's at least one—usually two or three. Each time they report:

- ☐ Board meetings resulted from a strategic initiative, not commodity product sales.
- ☐ One of the *Four Things Buyers Buy* was involved.
- ☐ The meeting gave them a tremendous sales advantage.
- ☐ In most cases, they were able to maintain executive relationships after the meeting.

I too have met with various board members. In each case, my

security insights gave me access to the board. My assessments have frequently led to invitations to attend meetings, speak at conferences, and provide counsel to those leading the company's strategic initiatives. There is power in understanding security at a business level.

Large manufacturers like IBM often gain access through their brand, but it's a rarity for the average salesperson. Leaders want to know how secure their companies are. If they're convinced you can help them, they will invite you.

A Powerful Door Opener

Security is a powerful door opener. As a salesperson, I want to control the sales process. To do that I need an offering that truly matters to decision makers. I need a way to shorten the sales cycle and maintain a competitive advantage. I want to become a trusted advisor to the companies I serve, ensuring our relationship is lasting and mutually profitable. Security does this.

Having relevant security knowledge will allow you to become the go-to expert for companies that are trying to avoid information theft-related exposure, lawsuits, embarrassment, and fines. And because security intersects with IT disciplines like networking, data center, cloud computing and mobility, you can anticipate requests for your input on all types of business initiatives. In fact, the WSJ recently reported the CIO as being involved in every major business initiative because technology is central to just about every decision being made. And where there is a technology change, there's a need to review, and often enhance, security.

I'm convinced that security creates a new value proposition. It offers greater access potential than any other product or service. Neither an engineering background nor a highly technical security background is required to sell/advise at the buyer level. Of course, you'll want to have some engineers to back you up when things do get technical.

A Business Multiplier

With security's measurable growth over the last decade, why do so many companies fail to profit from it?

Companies approach security as a product sale, which raises all kinds of questions:

- ☐ Is there a return on investment?
- ☐ Can we afford this?
- ☐ How does this product compare to others we've seen?

This means the seller must justify the product, while facing comparisons and price pressure. The resulting installation projects are small, and the ultimate profit may not be worth the effort.

With minimal effort, however, you can use security as a value proposition, showing companies how they're being attacked, creating an opportunity where none existed. Over the course of this book, you'll gain an understanding of how to sell security to large enterprise accounts with big budgets and profitable ways to work with small companies that don't have an IT staff.

While working with a global manufacturer over the last year, I found that most security opportunities involved only one product/install per customer. Only a fraction of this company's security bookings came from 80% of its sales. But a few salespeople had figured out how to sell security, with more than 60 percent of security revenue coming from only 3 percent of the firm's sales opportunities. These talented professionals had discovered the right selling process—and you're about to learn the secret to making it happen for you.

CHAPTER THREE

The Secret to Selling Security Regardless of Budget

> The risk of losing one's most valuable assets is enough to force immediate action. At some point budget just doesn't matter anymore.

"We don't have a budget for these projects."

When I hear these words I know I'm talking to the wrong people about the wrong things. Companies reallocate when loss is eminent. So why is it so hard to sell security? Security problems are evident. So how do we capture this business?

Start By Redefining Security as a Discipline

First, most high-tech companies, both manufacturers and resellers, have made a strategic error in defining security as another practice area. Offerings like unified communications, storage solutions, enterprise systems, application development, and data center, have encouraged technology companies to treat security as a product when, in fact, it is not. Security is a discipline.

Let's assume you're going to buy a car. Would you purchase one without safety features and then hire a special auto safety company to add the necessary components? Years ago, when security simply wasn't part of the core infrastructure, a similar mindset might have been acceptable. Not today. While automobiles have many add-on safety features, their basic structure includes safer frame design, panel design, security glass and meticulous engine placement to reduce injuries in head-on collisions.

These safety features aren't treated as post-sale add-ons. In fact, many consumers consider safety to be their top priority when shopping for a car; just ask any Volvo owner. **In the computer world, security is analogous to car safety, not auto insurance as it is most often compared to. Insurance is an add-on, and nobody wants to buy more than they already have – in fact, we're all looking for another opportunity to "Save on our car insurance".**

Security is a discipline that must be applied to all technology, just as safety is built into the automobile. Cisco and Microsoft—companies that own the majority of corporate America's networks and operating systems, respectively—are working hard to build security into their products.

It's not hard to visualize every router and switch having firewall, intrusion detection, spam filtering and anti-virus software built into the network. And instead of installing several different products to stop viruses, spyware, and spam, they could simply be part of the operating system. Just look at the marketing behind Microsoft's newer operating system releases. It used to be about ease of use, now security is almost always mentioned.

In the storage world, EMC outperforms all other providers, with twice the market share of its closest competitor, IBM. What is EMC selling? Security built into the storage process. With acquisitions of Network Intelligence and RSA, to name just a couple, EMC has managed to build a company that stores and protects digital assets.

Security appliances are a stepping stone to integrated solutions. And while there are still many smaller firms building one-off security appliances, the technology giants like Cisco, EMC, and Dell are acquiring security companies and making them part of the core infrastructure.

The Truth About Security Budgets

Over the last decade, IDC studies show steady spending increases in security hardware, software and services. In the 2007 edition of this book, security spending was as high as 11.4 percent. By 2014 it was estimated to be as high as 14 percent. By the end of 2014, JP Morgan was reportedly doubling their security budget after a massive breach. The growth continues as large companies are attacked and their names appear on the front page or our local newspapers. In summary, here's what we can expect.

Top Budget Increases

- ☐ Security
- ☐ Cloud
- ☐ Virtualization
- ☐ Wireless & Mobility
- ☐ Analytics
- ☐ Software designed to improve customer retention.

Top Budget Decreases

- ☐ Hardware
- ☐ On-premise software
- ☐ Data center consolidation
- ☐ Network services management
- ☐ Unified communications

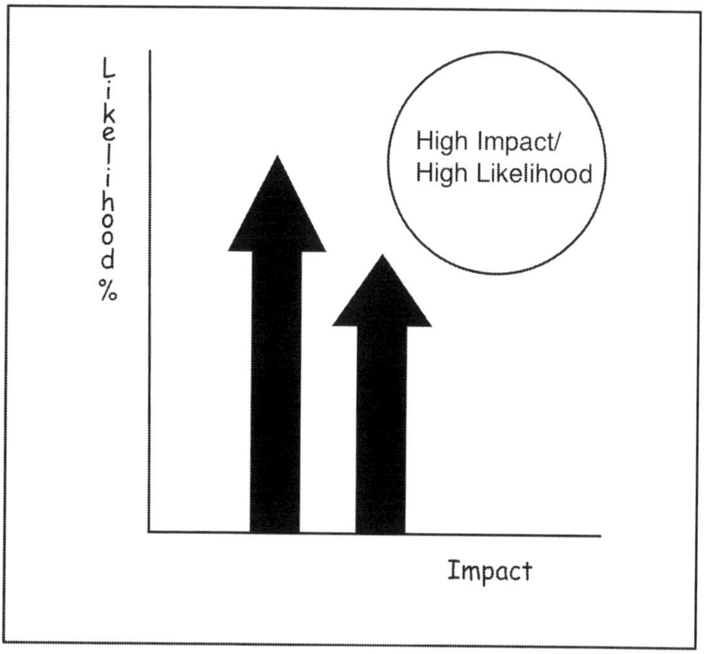

Figure: Justification For Change

- *Source: IDC*

A company's security budget often reflects how seriously it takes security. But don't let small numbers deter you from selling what the company really needs. Utilizing the car analogy, what if I could prove that your transmission will fail tomorrow? Most of us haven't set aside a special budget for transmission repairs, but we'll come up with the money needed to replace the transmission or the entire car. Even without a budget, we'll reallocate.

A better comparison is health. Later in the book we'll be talking a lot about a chart I refer to as the Impact vs. Likelihood chart – pictured above.

A few years ago I was experiencing some chest pressure. After a long night of worry I finally brought this matter to my wife. She immediately responded by rushing me out to the car, and racing off to the ER. My family has a history of heart disease, and a recent physical showed high cholesterol and some very high triglyceride numbers. My wife was in a panic, and I didn't feel very well.

Fifteen minutes later we were heading into the ER, signing in as a cardio patient, and suddenly the entire staff was focused on me. I was rushed down the hall on my back, IVs being inserted, tests being run, and papers being filled out. We were there all morning as a team of highly trained physicians and assistants withdrew fluids, ran tests, and analyzed results. Their assessment process was in full force looking for the root cause.

There was no discussion of time, money, or insurance. Not even lunch plans. But somewhere around the lunch hour, results were coming back, mostly showing encouraging results. While I hadn't felt well through the night, the tests confirmed that I was not having a heart attack, nor had I had one in the night. That didn't mean I couldn't have one right now, but there didn't seem to be any immediate indications. Still, they were monitoring closely.

As the morning was coming to a close the nurse came in with a semi-final report. The results looked good, but there were some possible issues that should be monitored overnight, and a stress test was ordered for the morning. The nurse informed us that the ER did not actually have an overnight facility, but that the ambulance would be arriving shortly to transport me to the hospital. Not until now had I considered my BCBS Insurance policy. Suddenly I wondered if they were going to pay for this transport.

My wife immediately got on her cell phone to find out. Had this been an emergency, they would have paid, but since this was considered a transport and not an actual emergency, there would be a $1500 invoice sent right to us with no coverage. Wow, $1500 for a 20 minute car ride? Looking over at my wife I said, "Maybe you should just drive me."

"O No," replied the nurse. "You'll need to take the ambulance, they're on their way."

I wasn't about to spend $1500. Right about now, with the tests all looking okay, I was feeling pretty good. In fact, had it not been for my wife's concerns I would have walked out and driven myself home. But my wife really wanted that peace of mind that comes with the doctor's final report. So I again noted to the nurse that I was going to the hospital, but not taking the ambulance. At that point she simply left the room to find the doctor.

It wasn't long before the doctor arrived, clipboard in hand, and ready to order me into the ambulance. After I brought up my concerns about the costs, she immediately went into a monologue on high impact risk.

"What about your family, your heart, your cholesterol, blah, blah, blah." What if I had a heart attack on the way over? Who would save me? She was right, the impact of such a crisis would be big! I have seven kids and a wife who depend on me to provide for them.

It was at that point that I had to bring out the impact vs. likelihood chart.

Impact runs along the X-Axis. I get that. It's bad if something happens on the way over to the hospital. But now let's go to the Y-Axis. This is the likelihood axis. It's the axis most sales people leave out. Everyone wants to talk about impact, impact, impact…and they're right. If something goes wrong, it's bad. But what's the likelihood?

When I arrived that morning, in my mind the likelihood was

high. I had symptoms, and according to my quick research on Google, my symptoms lined up with someone who might be on the verge of a heart attack. But now, with all of these professionals analyzing my heart, I was feeling much more confident that everything was going to be okay. I didn't object to more tests, but the $1500 car ride was not part of my security plan.

When a sales person can demonstrate high-likelihood, justification is clear. But when that Y-Axis is showing low probability (or is simply unknown,) suddenly the sale comes to a halt. Budget is not the issue, unless there just isn't any real justification. But once the likelihood axis looks high, budget suddenly fades into the background.

When your prospect starts bringing up budget, either they are the wrong person – meaning they don't actually have any liability in this matter, or they don't see a big likelihood. And most of the time, that is because you didn't provide one.

When the impact likelihood graph looks weak, the sales process tends to go back to price and compliance. Many companies have told me that their products would sell themselves, compliance would drive big profits, and security products would be the No. 1 expenditure. But the appliance market constantly simplifies the process, and companies buy the minimum solutions as they observe fewer viruses and other visible signs of foul play. Regardless of the true likelihood, when smart hackers are at work, there just doesn't seem to be much evidence of a problem.

Decision makers have become numb to the news stories and warnings. At the same time, a new appliance with a slightly different spin appears on shelves almost daily, saturating the market with cheaper, simpler solutions. Across the board, salespeople have become disillusioned with the prospect of closing big security deals. Not because the need isn't there, but simply because they have not learned to justify the sale.

Two Secret Weapons That Change Everything

There are two strategic keys to selling security. Understand them and you will completely tranform your sales process:

1. **Forget about products. Focus on the assets.**
2. **Find the asset owner.**

When you focus on the product, your audience is the technical team. Assets belong to the business and are the concern of decision makers—those with liability and ultimate responsibility. I refer to these as the Asset Owners. Sales consultant and author Mack Hanan once shared with me that these assets are the margin-sustaining element of any business. The last person you want to meet in the selling process is the IT security person who has no liability. Security people are just one of many influencers you'll engage later, once the deal is about to close.

In most meetings, you'll find two individuals: Asset Owners and data custodians. We spend most of our time with custodians – the IT people that watch over IT systems. Identifying the owner is the key to making the sale. The custodian has no liability or real decision-making power, but salespeople mistakenly spend countless hours negotiating, proposing and convincing them to buy. I'm not saying that the custodian has zero influence, but never give him the task of selling your solution for you. He's an unqualified salesperson.

If you wind up in a meeting where both the Asset Owner and Custodian are present, you need to make sure your focus remains with the Asset Owner. Sounds easy, but it's not. If a technical detail comes up and the custodian "wakes up," Asset owners will often bow out of the meeting – among them will be the actual economic buyer. You'll hear something like: "Why don't you folks continue and Bob can fill me in later today." At that point, you've lost control of the sales process.

That's why it's critical to find the Asset Owner and begin the process of helping him preserve his business early on – even before he knows there's a problem. Focusing on the product will sabotage your efforts, landing you a date with the data custodian.

So once again, forget about the products, focus on the assets, and find the Asset Owner. This is where the sale begins. From there, you'll work to understand Impact, but you'll continue your discovery process to learn more about likelihood. This is where justification will be found, and margin will be preserved.

CHAPTER FOUR

An Opportunity In Every Single Account

> Will your customers' current security strategy actually hold up under today's attackers? Understand your client's problem and how to identify real security opportunities.

Is there really a need for more security experts out there? Are your clients really in trouble, or do they have it covered? Are you qualified to advise them on security, or would you need to go back to school?

Every Company Has an Urgent Security Problem

Every client with important data has a security need right now! They may not know it, but they do. Your job as a sales person is to find it, show them, and convince them of the importance of taking action. This is why I love security. I know there's a need every time, so I don't have to look for people who have a need. I just need a way to convince those I know that they have a problem. This is unique to security sales. Everything else you sell only fits with certain companies, and discovering that need is time consuming.

How Long Does It Take To Lose Data

Several years ago I had the opportunity to travel to South Africa for a two-day sales training workshop. With no time for sightseeing, I grabbed souvenirs at the airport for my wife and children. This was the only purchase I placed on my personal credit card while in Africa.

About 20 hours later, upon arriving home, my wife greeted me at the door and informed me the bank had called repeatedly, requesting a return call as soon as possible. They would not tell her what the issue was, but indicated it was urgent.

"Mr. Stelzl, have you been in South Africa recently?" a representative asked when I returned the call. It seemed odd for the bank to know this, but of course I had.

"Did you purchase a large quantity of hydraulic equipment, in an amount approaching $25,000?" I was asked. "We have a record that someone made a card-present transaction of that amount just yesterday."

In other words, someone in South Africa had actually presented a card with my name on it to a merchant and made a purchase. This incident occurred at the beginning of the credit card-fraud and identity-theft trend more than ten years ago. At the time, I didn't understand how easy it was to duplicate a card, but today we hear about it almost daily. It takes just a few minutes to do it, and can be done across millions of cards with very little effort.

Understanding How Easy it is to Steal Data

This chapter explores how cyber-crime has evolved over the last fifteen years. Following this discussion I'll share with you how to leverage this data in the sales process. But first, let's understand the history and where we are right now. With this understanding it will be easier to spot an opportunity.

Scaring your clients into buying security has not worked. As a salesperson, you require a clear understanding of the security risks and how you can leverage them in your business. So the history side is important. Note, we are not selling anything yet, but rather gaining an understanding of what's out there. The facts in and of themselves won't lead to a sale.

The Changing Faces of Cyber-Crime

In 2007, when I first wrote The House & the Cloud, I cited that "about 12 computers in an average organization encounter some form of malicious program including viruses, spyware, botware or other malware, in any given week."

These numbers are probably more optimistic than today's numbers, but the threats are changing and growing in new directions, and that's where we'll turn our attention. In a 2013 Wall Street Journal article, a company in New York's financial district was under attack through social media - Facebook. A 25 year-old woman had reportedly contacted a large group of men in an investment company, *Friending* them one after another. The article goes on to report that over 75% of them gave her highly sensitive information over the course of the month they were involved. But get this, 13% of them gave her passwords…company passwords to financial systems! How does a company defend itself against this type of attack? These are authorized users giving out company secrets through social media to some young woman they've never met.

You might have already guessed, but it turns out that this 25 year-old woman was actually a 40 year-old man, working as a white hat hacker. He was hired by the company's leadership team to test the integrity of the company's end-users. Obviously they failed the test.

These statistics highlight generally visible security problems, but they are not necessarily the most damaging. Managers would like to eliminate them, but are unwilling to spend more money. In many cases, viruses have been handled adequately with antivirus applications. End user awareness training on the other hand is generally lax, yet it's the people that represent the greatest problem.

Since my trip to South Africa, credit card fraud has accelerated, and credit card numbers are a dime a dozen. But the problem has escalated to information theft in a much bigger way. Some of the most damaging instances now involve espionage and government systems infiltration. And as of this writing, there have been numerous instances around the world of disrupting critical infrastructure such as energy and financial systems.

So Easy - Kids Can Do It From Their Cars

You might remember reports as far back as 2004 when Brian Salcedo, age 20, pleaded guilty to four counts of wire fraud and unauthorized access to a computer. Apparently he and accomplices Adam Botbyl and Paul Timmins used an insecure wireless network at a Lowe's store in Southfield, Michigan, to steal credit card numbers from a point-of-sale system. Salcedo and his friends first stumbled across the network the year before, while driving around town, using their laptops to locate wireless Internet connections (a practice known as "war-driving"). Upon finding the Lowe's network, they hatched an idea.

Working out of Botbyl's Pontiac Grand Prix, the group began working on ways to access the company's systems, allowing them to "skim" each card swipe as purchases were made at stores around the country.

The method of their attack was facilitated by the custom software Lowe's used to process credit card transactions. The hackers downloaded and modified the software, creating an almost undetectable tool for "skimming" these card transactions.

On Nov. 5, 2003, Salcedo and his pals used a common Trojan program, readily available online, to gain access to Lowe's credit card transactions. Their modified TCPCredit program (the application used to process credit card transactions) was unsuccessful at first, but they managed to "crash" several point-of-sale systems at the local store. These system failures alerted the Lowe's IT department to investigate, which then led to FBI surveillance.

Two days later, the FBI team observed Brian and an accomplice using laptops and two suspicious antennas mounted on their automobile. This time, the hackers' attempts to install the modified TCPCredit software were successful and they began to skim credit card information as each purchase was made.

As they watched, FBI agents could pinpoint what was happening by reviewing Lowe's log files at its North Carolina data center. Only six credit card numbers were actually captured that night, but had Lowe's failed to recognize that something suspicious was occurring, every customer might have been forced to order new credit cards. But the major financial damage would have been realized on the Lowes side.

Target, 40 Million Cards Later, Does Not Have It Covered

You would think this type of attack would be over. There should be new security techniques or tools to stop it. It's still happing. In 2013, about ten years after Brian and friends captured their six credit cards, Target reportedly lost 40 million cards. In addition, about 70 million more identities where compromised. What's going on?

Target is Paying for This One

In the case of Lowes, only six cards were stolen. It was an amateur job, concocted in a car while driving around with nothing better to do. It took Brian and his friends about six months to actually steal the data. In my opinion, they probably accessed this network for fun at first, and then conceived their plan to do something with it. Their early attempt was weak, and of course they were caught through their own carelessness.

Target is a whole different story. In addition to the 1.4 million dollars, they reported a 6% decline in their fourth quarter sales forecast, and about a 20% decrease in earnings. They've been hit with lawsuits, and news reports have revealed customers saying they're done with Target. For the next three years, Target will be providing free credit reports to anyone who wants one, as long as they have shopped at Target. I'm one of them.

Dissecting The Target Attack

Interruptions. In the late 1990's I was running the daily operations of a 75 Million Dollar Reseller. It was busy. Each morning I would head into work with a million things on my mind. I made it a point to arrive early – before the chaos hit. My planner was my best friend. Mapping out the day, confirming meetings, checking on metrics and project status, new employees starting, problems to follow up on…a million things had to be scheduled. 30 minutes later, I had a plan…**plans are great, until the day really starts. Suddenly, everything is an interruption.** So what emergencies will actually get my attention today?

This is exactly what happened at Target. Executives in the retail sector are scrambling to compete with Wal-Mart; the unstoppable "Big Box" retailer.

Target is Wal-Mart's number one competitor. They're racing to catch up every day and suddenly some guy from security is down the hall yelling, "We need to do another assessment." He wants to know if someone can fund this. But no one's listening to him – online sales, cloud services, big data analytics, and social business trends are eating his lunch, as executives consider new business models. Target even had detection technology in place that could have stopped this – but it was not turned on. Huh?

This might be one of the most important marketing concepts I'll cover in this book. When company leaders are under fire for sales performance, they don't have time for security, and the security team will not be able to get their attention. You need something else.

We'll be talking more about what to do later in the book, but here's the thing, Target had a major problem and one of the security analysts knew it. However, even in the face of something seemingly urgent, he couldn't get their attention. Not only that, but you have to believe there were sales people in there from both large manufacturers and resellers. Target is a big company. It's a named account for someone, yet none of the sales reps calling on Target were able to get the attention of the decision makers. Something's very wrong here.

The other important lesson here has to do with the type of attack. We're talking about one of the largest credit card thefts in history. Was this a highly sophisticated attack? The answer is no. A little over ten years after Brian Salcedo attacked Lowes with a simple program change, this group came in through Target's HVAC maintenance company. With the trends of putting everything online, "The Internet of Things, (IoT)" criminals were able to gain access to the HVAC company's systems, weaving their way into the Target POS network. From there, they navigated through Target's PCI Compliance network right to the machines that read the credit card swipes. While segmentation was recommended, the cost or effort was too great. $1.4 million dollars later they are probably rethinking their priorities. The CIO resigned four months later; followed by the CEO! Meanwhile Target executives suddenly had several new and costly initiatives underway.

Compare Target, 40 million card loss top the 6 cards at Lowes.

Salcedo's actions at Lowes resulted in about $2.5 million in damages. Salcedo was quickly caught and later sentenced to 19 years in prison. Target's damages are much greater. Later in the book we'll look at the real difference here. It turns out that Lowes got lucky in that they moved to a new strategy, one that Target didn't have in place. But it was purely accidental. We'll talk more about that shortly.

Ignorance Is a Big Part of the Problem

Just recently my office manager was setting up travel for me to speak at Westcon's Beyond Security conference in Park City, Utah. In the process of scheduling transportation to and from the airport with the hotel concierge, we received back a confirmation email. I'm sure the hotel has a firewall – maybe a great one! But the email they sent contained just about everything a hacker would want to know about me – including my entire credit card number and expiration date.

I responded by contacting the manager over concierge services. Naming the person who sent the email, I was told that the sender was new to the resort and had made a mistake. Not completely happy with this answer, I asked him if he knew why this was a problem. His response was about half-right.

He seemed to get the fact that people can see email content. Pressing further, I asked him if he understood what PCI Compliance was, what a violation would mean to his hotel, and how Visa might respond if I were to put a call into them. He was clueless. Somewhat enjoying this conversation (despite the fact that my credit card is probably posted on various websites around the world by now,) I mentioned my upcoming keynote on security at his hotel. I noted that this might make an excellent example. Again he apologized and we ended the call.

Stories like this one create opportunities. The business side managers are liable for what their employees are doing. If this type of thing creates a real problem, it's going to cost the company money – big money. Companies can't afford this. And it's far more expensive than your proposals to fix it. But you can't sell this to IT. It's time to move out to the business units. I'll talk more about this in the next chapter.

Company Secrets, The Newest Hacker Targets

Credit card theft has been around for a long time. It's still a problem. But what about company secrets – the ones that keep your clients ahead of the competition and growing? How much is it worth to keep a company's next invention under wraps? Credit card theft is nothing compared to a company's ten year R&D effort going overseas to be copied.

"**Hackers target startups that secure early-stage funding.**" This headline appeared in a recent WSJ article, showing that startup companies are now detecting cyberattacks just after they raise their Series A funding. In other words, hackers are monitoring these companies to see when the funding is made available, knowing that there will be a sudden influx of cash available. They might also be after a start-up's new development or invention; something that might lead to a large payday for the hacker. Business leaders tend to disregard this kind of news because their IT people are telling them, "We've got it covered." Recently I spoke to a group of CIOs in Irvine California, hosted by a nationwide reseller and McAfee (now part of Intel Corporation.) This is a message every business leader needs to hear, before it's too late.

Recent Patent Law changes encourage the theft of intellectual property when it deals with innovation. The person who files first has an advantage over the patent right. That means that as your clients are inventing, others are watching online to see when a development is ready, but not yet filed in the patent office. This would be a good time to strike.

Notice that the security risks are suddenly higher at this point. Back to the Impact vs. Likelihood graph I referred to earlier, the measurement of impact goes up, but so does the likelihood of attack. Understanding this is key to building a solid security architecture – it is also critical for the security provider if you want to better understand the sales cycle and how to justify a change in security spending. Again, we'll be covering this in more detail later.

Chinese Government – Are They Really Hacking?

What about China? There have been numerous hacker reports on the Chinese Government over the past year. Are they really hacking into US companies? I have not personally experienced this – however the news is certainly saying, "Yes".

"The disclosure early this year of a secretive Chinese military unit believed to be behind a series of hacking attacks has failed to halt the cyber intrusions," according to Reuters's Deborah Charles and Paul Eckert report. Wall Street published this in November 2013, pointing to the People's Liberation Army - Shanghai-based Unit 61398 – the primary suspect. This sounds pretty specific. What are they after?

According to the above mentioned article, this effort involves "cyber espionage to steal proprietary economic and trade information," from the U.S. In other words, they are after U.S. innovation; stealing what has taken years to develop, with a plan to take U.S. innovations and manufacture without the upfront R&D cost. Expect these new products to come on the market for much less, competing with the inventor on price. This is called a *copycat* product, and often puts the inventor out of business.

If your clients are still thinking they are safe, have avoided attacks, and have *it covered* when it comes to keeping their innovation secrets under cover, they're likely out of touch with the real world. IT has often said, "*We have it covered*," only to later find out that hackers have been inside for years. Again, the FBI says it takes 14 months on average to discover an attack, but many companies will never figure it out until it's too late.

"U.S. Eyes Pushback On China Hacking"

This came from a recent headline in the Technology section of the Wall Street Journal. One interesting perspective from a news reporter explains that these attacks are "small enough for our government to ignore them." In other words, there is no one single incident big enough to demand a government level response. This is important. It's a way for one country to attack another without actually going to war. Another article in that same section warns us that, "All major U.S. companies have been successfully compromised…" Where is this all headed?

Companies who insist, "They've got it covered…" are in trouble and kidding themselves. No company is impenetrable. In fact, the idea of using a pen-test to show your clients that their data is safe only delivers a false sense of security. A failure to break in simply shows the incompetence of the pen testing team. It certainly doesn't mean the company is well secured.

In a recent report from the U.S. President's office we read, "The Obama administration is considering a raft of options to more aggressively confront China over cyberspying,…, a potentially rapid escalation of a conflict the White House has only recently acknowledged." The key phrase here is, "Only recently." Why have government officials denied this for so long? Perhaps for political and economic reasons. The Journal states it like this, "Before now, U.S. government officials and corporate executives had been reluctant to publicly confront China out of fear that stoking tension would harm U.S. national-security or business interests."

Why are the Chinese on the attack? "China is stealing trade secrets as part of plans to bolster its industry," (WSJ). It's simple, the U.S. has a greater capacity for innovation. By invading a company's intellectual capital, other nations can cut thousands of man-days out of the R&D process. Google, EMC, RSA, New York Times, Wall Street Journal, and many other well-known companies, along with many federal organizations including the Pentagon, have reported problems that can be traced back to China. However, things like "dependency on China to underwrite U.S. debt and to provide a market for U.S. businesses," have allowed these nation-state sponsored attacks to go unchallenged.

Following are some hard hitting news quotes regarding China:

- "If the mission were to change, they [Chinese Hackers] have all the tools in place to destroy…" - WSJ
- "Chinese military unit 61398, is believed to be behind the theft of hundreds of terabytes of information from 141 organizations primarily in the United States." – SC Magazine
- "Mandiant named the group APT1 –…it is only one of dozens of advanced persistent threat (APT) groups with China-based operations that the firm tracks." - WSJ
- "Industries targeted by APT1 also match industries that China has identified as strategic to their growth,… identified in its 12th Five Year Plan." – Department of Homeland Security. (Reports show that this has been going on for 12 years, and that 12 major industries are targeted in these attacks.) - WSJ
- "The size of APT1's infrastructure indicates that hundreds, and possibly thousands, of people work for this group, including linguists, open source researchers, malware authors, industry experts..." – Department of Homeland Security. - WSJ

Your Country's Biggest Problem

Recently U.S. government officials have come out saying, "Cybersecurity threats are the greatest threat to our security—economic security, political security, diplomatic security, military security." Note – this could be any country. No matter how big your customers are, cybersecurity is something you want to understand and engage them in. So even if it's not the CIOs number one concern right this minute, these reports underscore the importance of security. The challenge of using this issue as a door opener is simply a marketing problem. Everyone out there has the need.

CHAPTER FIVE

The Silent Killers

> Your clients may not see evidence of foul play, but inside every network you'll find major issues. In some cases the data caretakers have become numb to these problems. Because they're everywhere, the thought is, they're not hurting us. The IT team is wrong about this.

Major Issues – No Company Is Safe

We haven't sold anything yet. This information is just to get you thinking about how serious this problem is. In the next chapter I'll be addressing what I call, "The Power of Sound Bites" and how to use them in meetings and conversations with those you're selling to. For now we just want to gain a thorough understanding of the gravity of this issue. Don't ever leave a sales meeting believing a company has it covered. They never do.

APT (Advanced Persistent Threat)

You've probably seen the term, "Advanced Persistent Threat," or APT. What is this? The APT are groups of people that want in –

they are a "who", not a "what". This is an important concept. APT has been a buzzword in the security industry for a while now. It refers to extremely tenacious attackers. Google "Stuxnet" (a highly sophisticated attack targeting the Iranian nuclear uranium enrichment program,) and you'll start to get a glimpse of the control the hacker has over us. Or consider cyberwarfare attacks that have taken down power grids – they're seemingly unstoppable.

The APT is bigger than Malware. These sophisticated attack groups use newly developed hacking tools that hide in a company's computing environment. When the operator (hacker) sees an opportunity to surreptitiously extract or gain access to whatever systems or information they're after they'll strikes using a combination of tools including social engineering and botware.

In general, these groups want one thing: intellectual property. And they are not giving up until they have it. In other words, they are "Persistent." If they can't get what they want one way, they'll simply find another entry point—likely through an unsuspecting employee or third party supplier. If they have to, they'll pay off an internal employee to get the access they need.

The Most Powerful Hacker Weapon Available Today

Social engineering is perhaps the most undervalued hacker tool out there. Author Bruce Schneier points out, "Security is not a math problem, it's a people problem." People are the entry point for these attacks.

Kevin Mitnick, former hacker, and author of *The Art of Deception*, goes into great detail on how people are deceived and talked into offering up credentials for just about anything. Going back to the 25 year-old woman on Facebook, she talked 13% of the men into giving out their passwords. This is kind of attack will defeat almost any security architecture.

Social engineering is one of those terms that has been around for so long, people ignore it. Read Mitnick's book and you'll discover how just about anyone can be talked into giving up their most prized secrets. He shares stories of people sneaking into military installations, financial firms, and just about any gated facility simply by talking the night watchmen into letting them in or convincing an office administrator that they work directly for the chief. He talks about calling office workers with news from executive management, convincing people he's from IT support; becoming whoever he needs to be to get what he wants.

His point is this, most people trust the people around them. All it takes is knowing the right language, and a few key names and you're in. This kind of information is almost always available on a company website or annual report.

Office workers are overloaded with work – they just want to get the job done. Few people are going to sit there and argue. It's easier to comply and move on. When social engineering is used correctly as part of a vulnerability assessment or pen test, it's always successful. Any good team will get in – good or bad.

The Virus

Malware is an urgent issue. It's one of my favorite security topics because it is so overlooked. When I mention "bots" (That robotic code used to infiltrate end-nodes through infected websites and spam), I can almost predict a roll of the eyes from some of the systems engineers. However bots and viruses are not the same. So let's take a look at the virus first.

Years ago I was working for a bank in the IT department. On one early morning during the Christmas holiday season I was awakened by a call from my manager. We had a virus! In fact, the virus had been sent out with some software to several of our corporate lending clients. This happened in the late 1980s. Back in the days of small hard drives and 5 ¼ floppy disks.

The next thing I knew, we were all scheduled to fly nationwide, hitting every client office who used this software. The mission was to visit each company in person, explain that we had a software update that needed to be performed, and secretly run a virus scanning tool to find the virus and delete it from the system - without the customer knowing about it. It was urgent, under cover, and costly to fix. But we did what was needed to address the issue.

Viruses have changed. They sneak in through all kinds of software updates, spam email, and infected webservers. But they are so common that most companies treat them as a normal occurrence that is easily handled by antivirus software. No one is getting on a plane to carry out a top secret mission to disinfect a PC anymore.

Think of a virus as something that spreads like a human virus, through some kind of contact, and seeks to destroy something. That might be overly simplistic, but for those who sell security, the target audience for this book, that's as far as we need to go.

Robots, Bots and Malware

Bots are not viruses. Perhaps a cousin, but not the same thing. The bot is more like a robot (which is where the name bot comes from). It seeks out it's target, secretly installs on the system, and reports back to the owner. But in reality, not all bots are malicious. So what is a bot really?

Wikipedia says it like this, "An **Internet bot**, also known as **web robot**...or simply **bot**, is a software application that runs automated tasks over the Internet." That's pretty generic and harmless. In fact, many bots are used by legitimate companies for legitimate purposes.

They are small software routines used to perform simple, repetitive tasks. Wikipedia states that "The largest use of bots is in web spidering. Simply put, an automated script fetches, analyzes and files information from web servers." So when you put up a new webpage, a bot program might be used to find it and index it in Google. Bots might even be used to crawl through sites like eBay looking for bargains.

Malware is the term that has come to mean any software with mal-intent. Malware is the superset that viruses are a part of. Malware also includes bots that do something illegal or destructive. (A recent off-shoot is malvertising – advertisements that contain bots.) Bots that fall into this category do a number of things. For instance, spambots are used to harvest email address from websites. Because of this, it is not a best-practice to list an actual email address on a webpage or blog post. Other bots might be used to cripple a server's bandwidth by downloading an entire website (called a downloader program), or by creating so much traffic that a given company's servers are overrun with requests (in this case being used as DDOS or Distributed Denial of Service Bots). The DDOS attack most often originates from hundreds or thousands of bot infected computers, working together in the form of a botnet. And one last example would be a web scraper. Scrapers are bots used to find a certain type of content online, with the mission to steal it (or scrape it) and repost it somewhere else (which often represents a copyright violation.)

With most bots, there's no announcement or "destructive payload" (A term used for a bot that carries with it some destructive virus-like function.)

Bots have been around for many years, and have been the number one tool used by hackers to gain access to systems and data (usually in conjunction with social engineering tactics that convince people to do something to allow the bot to install.)

The Urgency of Bot Infections

Just about every company has systems infected by bots. I say, "Just about," because I can't prove that everyone has one. But I don't think I've ever been through a comprehensive assessment project and not had the team uncover at least one.

Unlike a virus, the bot only needs to be planted on one computer to do major harm to that organization. Is it urgent? Most technical people I run into don't see it that way. When they enter into an assessment project, they are looking for the cooler, more sophisticated attack vectors. But when I explain to a company president or CFO what a bot really is, in layman's terms, they seem alarmed by it. It goes something like this:

"If I were to tell you that someone from outside your company, someone you don't know, has installed some software on your personal computer, and now potentially has access to all of your files, your data, your connections to your personal bank account, and more, would that be urgent? What if they could hear your conversations through your PC mic, and even see you through your built in camera? Would that be urgent?"

When a business person hears this, they immediately think it's urgent. This comment leads to project work in a single day. In fact, I have had numerous clients call me back to let me know this landed them billable work that afternoon! It's that urgent.

The broken pipe analogy makes it clear. Imagine you're at home and you suspect a leaking pipe in the wall. You call the plumber to investigate. An hour later he shows up, runs through a few assessment procedures (this is your vulnerability test), and comes back with bad news. It looks like your pipe is leaking. At that point he lets you know he is headed back to the office and will work out some options, some pricing, and get a proposal out to you by Monday. How do you respond? Do you thank him, or do you call another plumber?

It's urgent, right? You're not going to wait till Monday while there's water leaking in your wall. You know that sheetrock is going to disintegrate quickly, and that your house will be flood damaged property just a few hours from now. It's urgent.

Your bot might be a simple marketing bot put on there to collect information, or it might be a team of Nationstate Sponsored hackers infiltrating your company. You don't really know. In most cases it would take a lot of expensive investigation to find out, so the safe thing to do is stop it! Delete it, clean it, do whatever must be done; prevent further infection.

"Malware is going undetected for weeks or months," reports the Wall Street Journal. 14 months is the average, according to 2013 FBI reports. That's over a year! Imagine letting your leaking pipe go for an entire year. I'll talk more about how to leverage these types of issues in the chapters to come.

SMB Companies – Prime Targets for Hackers

Do you call on small medium businesses (SMB)? Clearly the larger companies are being hit constantly by hackers, but what about smaller companies? The common belief out there is that the SMB company is not at risk.

Don't ignore security if you work in the SMB market. I continue to see smaller resellers focusing on managed services, but neglecting the security side of this program. Don't do it. Managed services contracts justified on security remain the most stable contracts for long-term recurring revenue. And while traditional managed services programs are quickly commoditizing, security isn't.

In a recent WSJ article, *Cyber Thieves Hit Owners*, the writer shows how small businesses are often held personally responsible for financial losses caused by hackers. While an individual can usually recover from a fraudulent wire transfer, for instance, it is only on some recent cases that the bank was held responsible for small business losses. While the writer takes the positive side, seeing a trend to help small business, the laws don't normally favor the small business owner.

Every project, regardless of size, should incorporate security. And every reseller should assume their SMB clients are clueless about security. That's just the way it is, and this article says exactly that. Consider these sound bites from the articles above:

- ☐ "The proportion of those attacks that were explicitly focused on small business rose to more than 30%..."
- ☐ "The total number of targeted attacks on *SMB* organizations rose to an average of 151/day..."

Make sure you have security built into your discovery process. Look for weak end-node security, poorly configured firewalls, unstructured data outside the firewall, insecure web applications, and personal devices full of sensitive data lacking passwords and encryption.

Following is a list of sound bites I used in a recent SMB lunch & learn to convert over 90% of the 65 business owner attendees.

- ☐ 77% of SMBs say their company is safe from cyber-threats, such as hackers, viruses, malware or a cyber-security breach.
- ☐ 88% of SMB companies have no formal cyber security plan in place today!
- ☐ 73% of respondents said that a safe and trusted Internet **is critical to their success**.
- ☐ 59% admit that they do not have a contingency plan outlining procedures for responding and reporting data breach losses…which makes you wonder about the 73% cited above.
- ☐ 66% stated they are not concerned about cyber-threats (external or internal), such as an employee, ex-employee, or contractor or consultant stealing

data...(even though the WSJ reported last year that 75% of employees admit that they steal company data!)

- ☐ 86% said they are satisfied with the amount of security they provide to protect customer or employee data.
- ☐ 83% said they "strongly or somewhat agree" that they are doing enough or making enough investments to protect customer data.

Notice the inconsistencies here. But then, in an article published around the same time frame, Visa found that SMB represented more than 90% of the reported credit card breaches, and Symantec found that almost 40 percent of the more than 1 billion cyber-attacks prevented by Symantec in the first three months of 2012 targeted companies with **less than 500 employees!**

Obviously there is a disconnect here. Your first task, if you call on the SMB market, is to educate business leaders. Show them what they are up against, and how to tell if they are really secure. This is not about selling more product, it's about helping these business owners understand and get what they really need. Start with education and the product sale will be much easier.

More Alarming Sound Bites

Again, I'll be talking more about how to use sound bites in the next chapter, so these "bites" are just to get you thinking about security. Don't just start using them without reading the next chapter. Used improperly, they'll just get you into trouble.

Following is a list of alarming sound bites from recent business-related articles:

- ☐ "Executives were told the networks aren't connected,…it's not entirely true" This is one of my favorite quotes from a cybercrime report. Isn't that so often the case – senior management is in the dark on how things are connected! – WSJ.

- ☐ "Internet-based attacks on critical U.S. energy infrastructure are occurring at a greater rate than previously understood..." – WSJ.

- ☐ "The Department of Homeland Security, found that thousands of control systems used in critical infrastructure are linked directly to the Internet and are vulnerable to attack" – WSJ.

- ☐ "The team has been tracking threats and responding to intrusions into infrastructure such as oil and natural gas pipelines and electric power organizations at an alarming rate" – WSJ.

- ☐ "On average, malicious software infections are not discovered for 15 months, according to ICS-CERT. That leaves hackers plenty of time to do damage." – WSJ.

- ☐ "Four Russian nationals and a Ukrainian have been charged with running a massive scheme that involved hacking more than 160 million credit and debit cards from 2005 to 2012 – CNN.

- ☐ "52% of breaches involve some kind of hacking, 76% of network intrusions exploit weak passwords…, 40% involved malware, and 13% involve those with authorization – performing unauthorized activities - Verizon Crime report.

- ☐ "92% of breaches reported in 2012 we perpetrated by outsiders. 14% were committed by insiders. 19% were attributed to state-affiliated actors, more than a 10% jump from 2011" – VBDBIR.

- "When they hack into a system, they do have the ability to crush the system…I think they're there to steal the data." – WSJ.

The Bottom Line On Opportunities

It doesn't matter whether a company is big or small, and it doesn't matter whether they think they are safe or not. There is an opportunity to further secure every company out there. They might like their current provider, but there is still a security project to be had in every company. There is amazing power in knowing this. There is no lack of need or opportunity out there when talking security.

Suddenly, security is a sales and marketing problem, and nothing more. **You only need to perfect your ability to get in, and you know there's an urgent need sitting on the other side of the table.** Figure out how to grab the attention of the decision makers and you're on your way to new business.

On the other hand, never leave a company believing there just isn't an opportunity. Instead, when facing rejection, realize that they either really like their current provider, or your message is just too weak. Over time, with the right marketing strategy, you can get in.

CHAPTER SIX

The Power of Sound Bites

Sound bites are power-packed quotes and statistics that build credibility, while at the same time, negate push-back from IT and other inside blockers.

I discovered the sound bite years ago while delivering an executive keynote at a luncheon. There I was, deep into my story of scary trends and cybercrime happenings, when one of the more technical attendees, (who snuck in under the pretense of "CIO") asked a challenging, keynote-derailing question.

Rather than argue with her, I simply quoted a couple of facts and statistics from The WSJ. The response was more powerful than I could have imagined. She simply shrunk back in her chair and nervously made a few notes on her paper. She didn't ask any more questions. It was like I had hit her with a disabling nerve gas or something. Victory!

The more amazing thing was the other attendees' response to this little disruption. They seemed to appreciate what I was saying. In fact, one attendee later commented on this woman's question, noting how disruptive it was. The power of answering with a WSJ "sound bite" was evident. The IT leaders in that room respected what I was saying because I was quoting from their trusted source. This technical person had no idea what I was saying. It was obvious; she doesn't read the WSJ. That day I was sold. Quote from business sources like the WSJ and IT can't really challenge you. I've come to refer to this as "The Security Sound Bite". It's simple, powerful, builds credibility, and defeats just about any attempts from "IT Blockers" (Those who would stand in your way as you seek out security opportunities.)

She did later admit that she was not a CIO, and was in fact the IT administrator of a local firm who just wanted to learn more about security trends. Basically, she lied on her registration form.

It's amazing to me how powerful a sound bite can be. However, using a sound bite incorrectly can also set you back. While sound bites do build credibility, and they do defeat the challenging IT person's derailing comments, they can also hinder the sales process.

How Do Sound Bites Hinder a Sale?

Chip and Dan Heath explain why in their book, *Made to Stick.* In a recent study cited in their book, they show how statistics vs. a story about one child dramatically changed the outcome of a campaign asking for charitable donations. In the study, half those asked to give are given sound bites as justification for the need. The other half are given a story to read – an emotional story about one person in need.

The results are amazingly different. "On average, the people who read the statistics contributed $1.14. The other people who read *the emotional story* contributed $2.38 – more than twice as much...one individual trumps the masses," writes the Heath brothers. Several more studies are cited showing similar results. Here's the conclusion they come to, "The researchers theorized that thinking about statistics shifts people into a more analytical frame of mind." When your prospect goes into an analytical thinking mode, they stop thinking emotionally. And the researchers the Heaths are quoting tell us that it was people's emotional response that caused them to give. Later in that same chapter Heath notes, "Belief counts for a lot, but belief isn't enough. For people to take action, they have to care." The conclusion here is that emotional response is critical to the sales process.

Left brain thinking is judgmental. While the sound bite is interesting to the listener, it leads to contemplation, not action. If what you're selling really is important, your prospect must come to care about it too. If they don't, they'll set it aside, giving their attention to other initiatives and leaving you to sell to IT. More on that later.

Sound Bite Timing is Critical

Later in the book I will be using sound bites in a simple sales process, but for one reason only; to defeat the objections brought on by IT naysayers. There are always those who creep into meetings with a mission to challenge and disrupt. The WSJ sound bite is the remedy.

Getting the buyer to act requires emotional appeal. They have to believe it and care about it. The sound bite should only be brought up briefly to build credibility or defuse a challenge. The rest of the sale should be emotional – following a storyline, not sound bites as I see in so many sales presentations.

Becoming the Go-To, Unchallenged, Security Expert

Who is the trusted advisor? It's an overused cliché these days; meaningless to most decision makers. Yet, there is something about the trusted advisor that is important. Executives need advisors. Anyone in a leadership position knows they need to surround themselves with advisors in order to stay current. So while the "Trusted Advisor" title is overused and meaningless, the function is still very real and extremely important.

There are two key ingredients if you want to become the real Trusted Advisor. They are,

- ☐ Trusted
- ☐ Able to advise

Let that sink in for a moment. Of course, both seem obvious; but among the sales people you know, how many do you really trust? I'm asking you to step out of your sales role for a moment and look at those who have tried to sell to you. The car sales person, the network marketing vitamin product reseller, or perhaps someone who came by to look at your hail-damaged roof. How many of these people were really honest in their selling process? In my book, *From Vendor to Adviser*, I talk a lot about trusted advisors. Here's a great definition of honesty and trustworthiness from the Character Training Institute – taken from my book, *From Vendor to Adviser*:

"Truthfulness is earning future trust by accurately reporting past facts." A lack of truth results in gossip, being too blunt or outspoken, disrespect, and being indiscreet.

- ☐ Commit to be honest.

- ☐ Make sure you are selling something you can be honest about.

- ☐ Greed often leads to deception. Replace a focus on money with a focus on meeting your clients' needs.

- ☐ Focus on relationships – this requires honesty.

Honesty is evidenced by consistency and accuracy in reporting facts and stories. Over time people will notice that what you say lines up with the truth. Commit today to be accurate in everything you say, and to disclose the truth without any deceit. Reporting the truth in a way that deceives the listener is not honesty and disqualifies you from becoming a trusted advisor."

Are you being trustworthy and honest? Most sales people are not. They've allowed greed to creep in, overtaking their desire to be honest, just to make their quota, or get that extra commission. This is a great way to destroy future sales and referrals.

Then there is the challenge of becoming the advisor. Here's what I wrote about becoming an advisor in the same book:

Becoming the Advisor

Great leaders surround themselves with advisors. Get to know any executive and you'll find that they have an inner circle of people advising them on all kinds of issues. Only through their advisors can they keep tabs on all aspects of their business, covering a wide range of topics for which they claim no expertise.

How do you become an advisor candidate? It was once said, "The friends you keep and the books you read will determine who you become over the next five years." Perhaps if this were written today the speaker would add, "The videos you watch and the websites you visit." In any case, it makes sense that you read the right material, learning all you can to interact and advise executives.

On the other hand, several executives have shared with me that they like to choose those who advise and work with them. When people over perform to impress or gain access to the inner circle, it often comes off as self-serving. Bad character is hard to hide, and a person's real intentions will eventually emerge. Here are some things you can do to improve your position as an advisor:

1. Read Great Business Books

I constantly get asked, "What do you recommend I read?" Few of the sales people that attend my workshops read anything relevant to business any more. This is sad. Think about the effort you put into school. If you attended college, even if you did spend time partying, you probably studied hard for tests, stayed up all night to prepare for finals, worked on weekends and holidays, and spent a ton of money and time just getting through the four year program.

After that, perhaps you went on to get your masters degree. You spent more time, more money, and sacrificed more of your personal time, to get a piece of paper. Now you are in sales. Your income potential is probably limited only by your own efforts and market conditions. You could be studying things that actually matter. You could be learning about sales and marketing, negotiating, trends, public speaking, and presentation skills. But if you are like most, you are doing the minimum – learning about the products you sell, and expecting your hard work to bring in the accounts. Selling is more than hard work. It's strategy and know-how. It's understanding people's needs, how they think, what moves them, and how to persuade them. If you are already doing these things – you're way ahead…if not, consider getting yourself on a personal development plan.

2. Coaching

Sports figures, and now even high school athletes, hire coaches. The executives you call on probably have business coaches (if you call high), and many executives have hired coaches to help them become great speakers. Mentoring is what I really mean. The coaching industry has altered some of the playbooks on us, turning business and life coaches away from giving advice; replacing it with reflective listening. My opinion is that you should have a coach who is similar to a sports coach. One who gives you advice as they watch and critique from the sidelines. Peer group input, like we see in the public school system, is largely a failure. On the other hand, personal mentorship and discipleship have been used successfully since the beginning of time.

3. Training

Training, while not as good as coaching, is important as well. There are many things you can learn online, such as news, product features, and methods. Like reading books, Google has become an invaluable resource, and blogs can provide laser focused insight on just about any topic. Soft skills, message delivery, and selling are better taught through interaction. Insist that your company keep you up to date and growing these skills. Like an athlete, without training you will slowly become less valuable and eventually be replaced by someone younger and more energetic. Don't get caught at age 50 without the very things younger people don't have: years of experience and invaluable wisdom. Some areas I recommend you pursue: selling, marketing, speaking, presenting, and time management. Of course, becoming an expert on security (at the WSJ level) is a must.

How often have you spent your own time and money on some form of training? The company should pay for it, but how hard are you selling your need? Training is so important. You should do just about anything to get it. Even if it means making a personal investment.

Learn the sound bites and you'll become the resident expert on just about any topic. You can't compete with the IT people on knowledge, however you can become the bridge between technology insights and executive management. IT rarely has an open communication channel with their executive team, so this is the perfect place to get plugged in. Stop trying to compete on the speeds and feeds of product features, and spend your time ramping up on global trends related to something that matters. In this case, information security is a great place to be. There's nothing much "older" than a year or two that really matters. Security is constantly changing. There's an abundance of news and new trends being written about every day. Armed with this type of information you'll find yourself in demand. It is this type of information that has earned me meetings at the board level.

What Makes a Great Sound Bite?

Great sound bites come from trusted sources. The IT person might be reading InformationWeek or some other free tech trade rag. I find resellers are more likely to be reading Wired or CRN, or maybe nothing other than product data sheets. Make the WSJ or USAToday part of your routine and start memorizing the sound bites. Why these two? Because most executives travel and get these papers delivered to their door each morning. And most business leaders subscribe to the WSJ. Even if they don't read it, they get it and they trust it.

So what makes a great sound bite? Here's an exercise from my *Making Money w/ Security* workshop. On day two I ask students to bring in sound bites from recent news and blog posts online. From there I go through them, evaluating them for effectiveness. Here are some samples I used in a recent workshop.

- ☐ **BITE**: According to the Sans Mobility/BYOD Security Survey over 61% of companies responding allowed employees to BYOD but less than 50% feel confident in their BYOD policies. – **COMMENT**: not a bad quote, all encompassing, and from a solid source (SANS). However, will executives recognize or believe the source? Probably not…I would not use it.

- ☐ **BITE**: "About 40% of people are not taking the most basic security procedures, like setting up a screen lock or putting software on the phone that could find the phone if it's lost or stolen. – Fox News" **COMMENT**:

This is good if we tie it to business and the BYOD movement…recognizable source, pervasive, and tied to what I would call one of the key initiatives out their for most midsized companies – mobility.

- ☐ **BITE**: "Companies know they're not spending anything close to what's needed to make their networks invulnerable to attack, according to a 2012 study by Bloomberg Government. – Bloomberg" **COMMENT**: Strong source – and while it's not that new, it's new enough to stand up to the passive attitudes we see out there. The trick now is to tie this to some method of securing, or a mindset to be adopted by organizations. If I can show them where companies are failing, I'll have a place to take this sales discussion.

- ☐ **BITE**: "China is stealing trade secrets as part of plans to bolster its industry." Wall Street Journal on April 22, 2013. **COMMENT**: This is a good sound bite – it's global in nature, speaks of an ongoing trend, and affects any company that stores mission critical information such as intellectual capital or trade secrets. It also comes from a source that speaks to executives – the Wall Street Journal. No one is going to question its validity.

- ☐ **BITE**: "LivingSocial.com, a site that offers daily coupons on restaurants, spas, and other services, has suffered a security breach that has exposed names, e-mail addresses and password data for up to 50 million of its users. 4/27/13 – Ars Technica Magazine" **COMMENT**: This one isn't bad…it's an identity theft sound bite which in my opinion may be too common, however 50 million is a big number. The other problem is the reference. No one reads Ars Technica – at least not the C-Suite as far as I know.

- ☐ **BITE**: "What most organizations do is overreact: they throw all of their efforts into that one incident and are not looking at what they should be looking at," says David Amsler, president and CIO of Foreground Security. "And worse, they don't have a playbook [for response]. It's so haphazard, and that's where they fall down." **COMMENT**: This one is good. It speaks to the security strategy and can be leveraged to up-sell the bigger picture. It's what Cisco would call the architectural sale – an opportunity to look beyond the immediate disaster, and over the entire enterprise to sure things up. One downside on this one, it's too long. If you can't quickly quote it, you'll lose your audience.

- ☐ **BITE**: "More than 90 percent of user-generated passwords, even those considered strong by IT departments, are currently susceptible to hacking, according to Deloitte's analysis." **COMMENT**: I love this one. It's quick, quotable, concrete (meaning visual), and from a trusted source…and it affects every organization, federal, commercial, big and small.

Good sound bites are short, factual statements, that come from solid sources. They communicate something serious, alarming, insightful, or amazing. They build credibility. **When a sales rep is armed with numerous sound bites from credible sources, they appear to be well educated, well read, and in touch with the trends.** Over time, having read and memorized enough sound bites, you'll sound like an expert. After all, knowledge is gained mostly through the study of good books. Isn't that what changed most of us over the four to six years we spent in college? Here's a quick summary of the process:

- ☐ Determine what you aim to be an expert in. What will you be a trusted advisor of? Let's assume it's securing mission critical information – the focus of this book.

- ☐ Study newsworthy sources and discover the trends – pick out the sound bites. "If you think U.S. Military computer networks are secure, think again." Security experts report to the U.S. Senate committee – March 23, 2012.

- ☐ Memorize the BITE – if you spend 15 minutes each morning, scan the news, and pick out just one, you'll have countless up-to-date quotes at your fingertips the next time you meet with a CIO.

- ☐ Use these sound bites to communicate truths to executives. Their IT people are telling them "We've got it covered." In fact, 71% of mid-size companies believe (because their IT people tell them), that everything is fine. 90% of Visa's reported fraud cases come from this same group, and the FBI tells us that it takes at least 14 months before people realize they've been attacked. Notice that when I put all this together in a short presentation, I sound like I'm the expert.

What did I just do? I defeated the IT person's argument by quoting the Wall Street Journal – that is the appropriate use of a sound bite. **Rather than bickering with IT about how secure they are, simply pull out a sound bite that suggests that they have been infiltrated, and that they probably wouldn't know – so how can they be sure?** Who will the executive believe? It's no longer my word against theirs – it's IT vs. The Wall Street Journal report, the FBI, DoD…etc.

Having been on many security sales calls over the past 20 years, I can attest to this strategy – it works. Executives don't trust sales people, but they don't trust IT either. They do trust experts. The Wall Street Journal, Gartner, etc. are all considered trusted sources that go far beyond my word or yours, and certainly beyond their internal IT people. Your job is the persuade, not argue. Persuasion is "Guiding vital truths around other's mental roadblocks," - The Character Training Institute. Discover the truths, memorize them, and then guide them around these roadblocks.

CHAPTER SEVEN

Inside the Mind of The Attacker

> Knowing who is out there stealing data, why, and how, can give you the advantage when trying to convince asset owners they are at risk.

Since about 2003 data risk has been accelerating. Prior to 2003, computer viruses were the threat, and most of them written to create havoc. The sudden change in 2003, what you might have read in the news as, *The New Face of Cybercrime*, popped up suddenly as groups around the world discovered a new way to make money (tax free money.)

It wasn't long after the Lowes attacks and Albert Gonzales being charged with infiltrating TJ Maxx, that a barrage of identity theft hacks began surfacing. *Secure Enterprise* magazine reported on countless new attacks, including unauthorized access to systems at ChoicePoint, DSW Shoes, LexisNexis, Polo Ralph Lauren and several universities, including Carnegie Mellon, Boston College,

Tufts and two University of California campuses. Ameritrade, Bank of America and Time Warner also reported losing data on tapes, exposing sensitive customer information like credit card numbers, social security numbers, and other information that could be used to create fraudulent credit. The Identity Theft Resource Center posted the names of nearly 150 companies that reported ID theft in 2005, with 57 million exposed customers. By the end of 2006, this number had reached almost 200 major organizations with nearly 100 million exposed customers.

It was during this time that USAToday predicted an increase in identity theft incidents that would top over 250 million exposed credit cards, and a data resale market over a trillion dollars in revenue, bigger than the worldwide drug trafficking industry.

Many of the affected companies reportedly had well-planned security strategies, 24/7 monitoring systems, intrusion detection programs and other safeguards. But they were no match for cybercriminals who always seemed to be one step ahead.

These companies were in the news because of their size and brand. But whether a large company, small company, or individual, we've all be affected.

The next time you're in a meeting with asset owners and custodians, and the custodian announces "we have it covered," remind yourself of these statistics. Assume your prospects are either ignorant or lying.

Who is Behind These Attacks and Who Are They Attacking?

Much of this came to light with a website called shadowcrew.com. This domain is no longer valid, and hasn't been since the first edition of this book in 2007. On May 30, 2005, *Businessweek Online* described Shadowcrew as an organized crime operation that used identity information to perpetrate fraud. The story read like a movie about Mafia criminals, including secret service agents working out of a high-tech command center, on a stake-out. Observed on 12 digital screens resembling a war-room, the cybercrime gang was being watched. Operation Firewall was created to track down and arrest a group of people trained in identity theft, money laundering, and the resale of stolen information.

"At 9 p.m., Nagel, the Secret Service's assistant director for investigations, issued the "go" order. Agents armed with Sig-Sauer 229 pistols and MP5 semi-automatic machine guns swooped in, aided by local cops and international police" The result; . "Twenty-eight members were arrested, most still at their computers".

According to BusinessWeek, these groups were winning: "They are stealing more money, swiping more identities, wrecking more corporate computers, and breaking into more secure networks than ever before." The damages from these groups continues to grow into the billions.

Online information brokers like ShadowCrew.com take identity information and turn it into cash before account owners can react. It would have been easy for Brian Salcedo to take the Lowe's credit card numbers, visit "hacker" chat rooms, and find brokers who, for the right price, would turn them into fraudulent cards. It's an astoundingly quick process that should not be underestimated.

The hackers behind these crimes often keep a low profile, and they take more information than they immediately use. This means suspicious activity may show up on consumer accounts months after a security breach, so people must monitor their statements. It's also important to recognize that many companies do not report losing data.

As a solution provider, your job is to understand how security crises occur and educate your customers. This means knowing the most recent sound bites and being able to effectively use them at the right time.

Customer ignorance is a boon to salespeople, notes Michael Bosworth, author of *Solution Selling.* When customers actually understand the problems they face, they frequently have a solution in mind, he says—one that any of your competitors can fill. It's also true that just about every mid to large company has an internal network administrator who gets paid to solve this problem, and would like to have *security* on their resume. Don't expect them to simply hand this over to you.

But when asset owners are unaware of the real threats—and you can demonstrate the level of risk they are facing—you have the perfect opportunity to act as a trusted advisor and promote the value of your solutions. Bosworth estimates 95% of the market is generally unaware of the big issues, allowing you to provide the necessary customer education. This starts with understanding who's behind the growing threat of information theft.

Who's Vulnerable to An Attack?

As defined by security experts and the ISC2.Org common body of knowledge, **a threat is "a party with the capabilities and intentions to exploit any vulnerability in an asset."** Vulnerabilities, in turn, are weaknesses in the systems that hold a client's assets that could lead to exploitation. Risk is defined as the possibility of suffering harm or loss—in short, a measure of Impact vs. Likelihood. All of these terms were defined years ago by military intelligence and law-enforcement personnel with expertise in counterterrorism.

When I served as director of security for a global consulting firm, I received call after call from security product manufacturers who wanted me to carry their product lines. Armed with the latest data, they were ready to show that companies could have been immune to recent attacks if their products had been on board. It was tempting to remind them that if companies had simply kept their Microsoft patches up to date, this would have prevented many of the malware attacks that have given cybercriminals access to sensitive data.

Hackers and their techniques are a moving target. Understanding how the landscape is changing, and who's behind the attacks offers clues to defending corporate systems.

In the 2004 Lowe's case, the attack was opportunistic. Salcedo's friends claim they were merely looking for an email access point when they stumbled upon the Lowe's network. This may or may not be true, but they likely did not intend to steal credit cards when they first discovered the network. Six months passed before they actually started skimming data from the corporate headquarters.

Today's hackers have an ever-increasing bag of tricks for cyber-breaking and entering, and they're in high demand around the world for their industry expertise. In fact many of them go on to jobs as security consultants after being prosecuted. Author Kevin Mitnik is one great example, One of Brian Salcedo's colleagues did the same.

Spamming organizations are also paying big money to create spam relay services to market all kinds of annoyances, from Viagra emails to hardcore pornography sites. Brian Kreb's recent book, *SpamNation* is an excellent resource if you want to understand what spam really is and how destructive it can be. Hacking is big business for organizations that need money and aren't concerned with the ways they get it.

Early hackers were described as the "spotty 14-year-old who just wants to show off to his friends." The new world is composed of attackers—many from Eastern Europe or Russia and China—whose goal is much more sophisticated than the thrill of breaking in. These people are in it for the money.

Consider some of these more recent sound bites:

- ☐ "Our systems are probed thousands of times a day and scanned millions of times a day," – speaking of government defense systems…WSJ

- ☐ "We are experiencing damaging penetrations — damaging in the sense of loss of information. And we don't fully understand our vulnerabilities," – WSJ

- ☐ "Hackers have already penetrated the U.S. electrical grid and have stolen intellectual property, corporate secrets and money, according to the FBI's cybercrime unit. In one incident, a bank lost $10 million in cash in a day." - WSJ

- ☐ "We're talking about terabytes of data, equivalent to multiple libraries of Congress." – WSJ

Organized crime is behind much of this. It's become a huge profit-rich industry with organizations that are centuries old and comprised of tens of thousands of members. In many cases these are the same people behind human and drug trafficking. In this case they've discovered a business that is less risky, and potentially more profitable.

9 million dollars in 12 hours, not a bad hourly wage,

RBS' U.S. Payment Processing Division provides us with a great illustration from just a couple of years ago. This was a sophisticated attack, and I expect to see it happen again. According to SC Magazine, "The gang evaded encryption on the network of RBS' U.S. payment processing division, raised the limits on the accounts, created 44 counterfeit cards, and hired a group of *cashers* to use the cards to withdraw more than $9 million in less than 12 hours from 2,100 cash machines across 280 cities worldwide." Not bad for a bunch of 20 something year olds – now headed to prison.

If your clients think they're secure, don't believe them. Encryption, passwords, firewalls, etc., they're no match for the creative hacker. Companies must move toward faster detection mechanisms, better monitoring, and timed response plans. They need security intelligence. In many cases your clients won't be able to afford all of this – that's where managed services come in.

Destroying Someone's Life With Child Porn

Here's another type of attack reported in the Baltimore Sun Newspaper. Perhaps this one was not money motivated, but it could be in the case of blackmail or extortion. It's a tale that should wake up any lethargic manager or business owner who tends to be unresponsive to security treats – the threat of losing everything, including personal reputation, family trust, friends, and their retirement fund. This seems like an easy attack…

- ☐ Malware was used to infect Micheal Fiola's computer (a former investigator with the Massachusetts agency that oversees workers' compensation).
- ☐ The installed malware then used Fiola's computer as a storage repository for child pornography – this is one of the fastest growing businesses on the Internet today.
- ☐ We don't know the perpetrator, but we do know that Michael was initially charged, lost everything, spent a fortune, and has not recovered.

Business owners need to understand how easy it is to do this kind of thing and how likely it is they'd be held liable. It would be difficult to prove the pictures didn't belong to the PC owner – after all, anyone charged would quickly say, "They're not mine"!

Using Malware to Steal From Small Businesses

Here's how it works. According to the Washington Post, "The scammers infiltrate companies by sending a targeted e-mail to the company's controller or treasurer". This would generally be a Trojan (malware), that when opened, surreptitiously installs software designed to steal passwords on the controller's computer. Money Mules (people who transfers stolen money for the hacker are often recruited on-line for what they think is legitimate employment) are then instructed to set up bank accounts, withdraw the fraudulent deposits and wire the money to fraudsters; the majority of which are in Eastern Europe"

It gets worse. According to this article, **businesses do not enjoy the same legal protections as consumers when banking online. Consumers typically have up to 60 days from the receipt of a monthly statement to dispute any unauthorized charges. Businesses have about 2 days!** Apparently, the banks spend a lot of money on protecting consumer customers because "they owe money if the consumer loses money"...but the banks spend less on the corporate accounts "because they don't have to refund the corporate losses." Make sure your clients understand this?

Hacktivists – A New Breed

Anonymous, Lulzsec, Anti-Sec,... these are hacktivist groups. Anonymous dominated cybercrime news in 2012 and 2013. Most of their attacks were against enterprise organizations including Visa, MasterCard, PayPal, eBay, and many government agencies around the world.

Anonymous in particular, claims to have exposed the personal data of more than 4,000 bank executives over the past two years. What drives these attacks? "It's typically because a group doesn't agree with something, or they want to embarrass an organization," according to Patrick Runald, director of security research at Websense Security Labs.

The big question for technology solution providers is, "Does this affect our clients if we call on SMB and mid-market accounts?" The answer is, YES! There are three important lessons every technology provider should understand and use in the security sales process.

Lesson One: Your Prospects Don't "Have it Covered"
Anonymous announced most of their attacks before attacking. Even with advanced notice, they were unstoppable. How many of your clients' IT groups are telling management, "We have it covered?" In other words, they believe, or at least claim that they are ready to stop an attack. They're not. None of them are.

Lesson Two: One Wrong Word Can Land Your Prospects in Bankruptcy
Anonymous "Didn't agree." So they attacked. Anonymous could be anyone. Taking a stand on any issue or producing a product someone doesn't like, suddenly justifies an attack. And because it is "Anonymous", no one is held responsible. This is a growing mindset. History shows an attack can put a company out of business.

Lesson Three: No Company is an Island
Hacktivists make it clear, "We don't care about collateral damage." With the growing adoption of cloud services, third-party processing, and universal connectivity – "The Internet of things (IoT)," we are all dependent on services such as Amazon or PayPal to maintain daily operations. No company stands alone. So who is really vulnerable? Everyone is. There is no company out there who can say, "We've got it covered."

What Are Hackers After?

Today's cyber-criminals are after three things: money, information and power. All non-hacktivists, in the end, focus on some kind of financial gain.

In a bank, money may be the target as programs skim money from accounts. For retailers over the past couple of years this is has been a daily threat. In just a couple of years we've seen Target lose 40 million credit numbers, Home Depot with a 57 million credit card loss, and many other notable wins for the hacker. In addition, identity theft may also be used to generate money by misappropriating names from these companies to apply for loans or create credit cards/other forms of credit.

More recent attacks focus on stealing intellectual capital. **"The Chinese government has a national policy of economic espionage in cyberspace. In fact, the Chinese are the world's most active and persistent practitioners of cyber espionage today,"** writes Mike McConnell, former director of national intelligence, secretary of homeland security, and deputy secretary of defense, in a 2012 WSJ article. Although recent WSJ reports point to Russian Hackers as potentially more advanced and more dangerous.

What is the impact of this type of large scale hacking? Obviously there is the money side, but this also cuts into jobs, competitive advantages, and even national security. McConnell comments on the cost, stating, "We think it is safe to say that *large* easily means billions of dollars and millions of jobs."

The Internet is the ideal medium for stealing intellectual capital, money, and power. Hackers can easily penetrate systems that transfer large amounts of data, while corporations and governments have a very hard time identifying specific perpetrators.

Hackers may use a botnet to infiltrate target systems. Large networks of zombies can be used for spamming. Illegal businesses can be set up to distribute child pornography. The point is, these criminals are not using their own computers to carry out these illegal activities but rather your clients'. At some point someone has to ask the question, who is liable for the crimes committed through these corporate owned computers?

CHAPTER EIGHT

How Can This Happen?

> Most business owners and executives don't really believe this will happen to them. IT is too scared to admit it's real and they don't "Have It Covered". Management is too busy to care...Until it's too late.

How Information is Stolen

Seven years ago the bot was the number one tool being used to break into companies. Hackers would use spam email and bot infected websites to infiltrate computers. And in just about all cases, social engineering was used to convince people to do something online that would result in the installation of a bot on their system. This bot infection creates what is called a Zombie Computer – a system that has been hijacked by an unauthorized user and set up for future illegal exploits.

Seven years later, the same tools are being used, but with much greater sophistication. In the Zombie computer, the original owner remains in possession of the computer and is likely unaware of the second user; however, the system can be redeployed in an instant, acting as a relay for an attack against government resources, breaking into banks, or committing some other crime that could be traced back to the owner's system.

At this point you might be tempted to think that zombies, or the malicious code behind these attacks is the problem. However there is more to it. It's a Trillion Dollar business (up from 67.2 Billion in 2007 when I wrote the first edition of this book.) And it continues to grow with little resistance. We're losing this battle.

It would be foolish to think that, with the release of Microsoft's latest operating system, or perhaps a new release of anti-spyware software, that criminals will pack up their business and go into something else. Cybercrime was expected to grow over 20 times within a few years back in 2007, and it has. Like drug trafficking, cybercrime is extremely profitable, and controlled by some extremely powerful people. At this point there doesn't seem to be an easy answer to any of this.

Well funded, the cybercrime gangs that are after this data have the ability to pay off internal employees to do everything from install malicious code on servers, to hiring bankers to help launder money. The simple act of opening up an ecard or downloading free music and videos may be introducing bots into a system. Once the Trojan is installed, it's "game over". The hacker is in and can easily hide from basic security tools. Since the first writing of this book this problem is exacerbated by the proliferation of BYOD – Bring Your Own Device initiatives. People are using their own unprotected computers (including smartphones and tablets) for corporate work.

Where Are These Zombies?

If you're wondering where all of these bots are hiding, they're likely in the companies you call on. They are on corporate computers, laptops, home computers and personal devices (tablets and smartphones.) The hacker's goal isn't notoriety; it's stealth resources and profitable crime.

In 2006 a study released by Microsoft revealed that an estimated 60% of all systems outside the corporate network contain bots. By 2008, Symantec had published numbers as high as 88%. Recent numbers from Kaspersky show similar results today. This means that between company desktops, traveling laptops, and smartphones, chances approach 100% that your customers are hosting zombie computers. Is this urgent? Too many technical consultants have dismissed this as hype.

But consider this, in executive language a bot means; someone from the outside has installed unauthorized software on corporate computers, and now has access to whatever is on the system's hard drive, as well as the potential of collecting passwords through key loggers. Whenever I say it like this, to an asset owner, I get a predictably urgent response!

Millions of Methods Boil Down to A Few Likely Attacks

While malware or bots and some form of social engineering seem to be the primary tools of the trade, it makes sense to get an overview of where the big attacks are taking place right now. This varies over time and may go up or down making this book less relevant during certain years, but the following list has been with us a for a long time – and it's probably going to stay relevant for some time. Either way, it's up to you to stay on top of the news, the trends, and the specific threats in the geographies and verticals you work with.

Point of Sale Systems

Target, Home Depot, Neiman Marcus, Michaels – these are all POS system victims. According to the 2014 Verizon Cyber Security report, 2011 was the year of POS attacks, but recently there's been a resurgence. RAM scraping is being used to grab credit card numbers as unsuspecting shoppers slide their cards through the card readers at check out.

In Target's case it is thought that a malicious software program, readily available online, was responsible for the attack that resulted in the 40 million credit cards being taken. In Home Depot's case it was a similar but different program doing the same thing. These retailers are completely vulnerable given the technology most of them are using.

These hacker programs sell online for somewhere between $1000 and $2,500 and were allegedly used in attacks against Chase, Capital One, Citibank, Union Bank of California, and Nordstrom. In other words, they are easy to get and easy to use.

Even though these retailers use antivirus programs, the malicious software was not detected. They are not viruses. In Home Depot's case, the malware was disguised to look like their McAfee security software.

Web Applications

Web applications represent on of the largest holes in most companys' perimeters. For reasons of cost and time to market, programmers often sacrifice security for functionality. Clients sacrifice security to control costs and convenience. Strong authentication is one obvious measure companies should be taking. But most people view this as a hassle and if not forced into it, will not choose to take the added step.

Web applications are compromised most often using one of two methods. Either through some weakness in the programming, such as inadequate data input validation – meaning you might be able to execute some type of code on an input screen, or by using someone else's login credentials – basically impersonating someone (sometimes referred to as pretexting.) Most of these attacks seem to be focused on gaining access, defacing websites, and taking systems down through a denial of service attack.

Insiders and Ignorance

Insider attacks might be operator error. Or, they might be someone inside cooperating with an outsider to gain access to trade secrets.

These attacks tend to be financially motivated. But I've noted in one of my sound bites that 75% of all employees (as reported by the WSJ) admit to stealing data. Insiders are a bigger threat than company leaders realize.

Stealing Computers – a New Kind of Data Theft

In a recent report from the WSJ, entitled, "A New Kind of CyberThreat," there's a report of a guy getting off the subway in New York City. As he exits the train he is tripped, someone grabs his phone and runs while a couple of thugs hold him back from the chase. Another article tells of a guy standing on a street corner using his smartphone. Someone punches him in the face and runs off with his phone while he recovers from the blow.

The device might be worth $200 with a two year contract, but the data likely carries a price of thousands or millions if put in the wrong hands. Other thefts involve devices missing from cars, homes, and offices.

I suspect most of these crimes result in black-market resale; a source of quick cash. But you don't really know. Toting mobile computers with sensitive data is a big risk. Every device should have some sort of "find-me" software on it. They should also be password protected, encrypted, and there should be some sort of safety net that provides the ability to wipe the data if stolen. Most smartphones have this feature – the question is, are people using them.

Mistakes and Operator Errors

Recently my mother-in-law was moved into an assisted living facility. After some unexplainable events my wife began investigating their drug administration practices. My mother-in-law's health seemed to be rapidly declining. Sure enough, her medication was being improperly administered.

Most of us trust the people running the computers. We assume our bank balances are right, and the cashier is computing correctly and handing out the right change. After all, he's a professional, right?

The fact is, errors are being made unintentionally. As more and more computers are introduced into highly repetitive and mundane jobs, it will be harder to hire people with high-end skills to do that work. Automation leads to boredom and mistakes. Like my mother-in-law's experience, the cost will be high for some of these mistakes, and will go unchallenged until someone who really cares gets involved.

Skimmers

These programs do exactly what the title suggests – they skim. This is what happened at Target and Home Depot. Most of them end up on ATM machines, taking people's card numbers and login details which are later used to steal cash. It's fairly easy to purchase a hardware skimmer that can be mounted to a fake or real ATM machine. Others are installed on card readers at the checkout stand.

Denial of Services

For years I've taught that this is no longer a big issue, but it's back. Organizations such as Anonymous have used the distributed denial of service attack to take down large companies, forcing them to either pay money or change a decision. In most cases these have been political rather than financially motivated. However one of my cloud service providers recently suffered an outage that lasted all week. These events are costly.

Espionage

Finally, espionage is the high growth issue out there. Stealing company secrets is highly profitable, whether it is for resale or to build a copycat product. The other big target is government. Stealing military secrets and spying are daily occurrences.

According to Verizon's recent security report, espionage has tripled over the last year.

Everyone Is a Target

So, who are the real targets? In short, any computer that can be used in a money-making scheme.

Spamming is a growing, profitable market for those who take the time to figure out ways to get their message out without exposing the sender. Targets include any computer that can be easily accessed for use as a spam relay, computers that can serve as soldiers in a zombie network, larger systems that can provide storage/processing, or any system that can be used to create money. Targets also include systems used to process credit card numbers such as the ones used in the skimming incident Target suffered. Systems that deal with money, such as point of sales systems, systems with innovation and research, military secrets, or whatever can be used or sold for a profit, are the focus of today's hackers.

In the next chapter, I'll address the impact and associated liabilities that may result from these security violations. If you can prove that cybercriminals are in the accounts you are calling on, there will be an opportunity. Your understanding of what's happening in the world of information security—and how it impacts the corporations you deal with—will allow you to create the security value proposition message for the uneducated buyer.

With the right messaging, your prospects will take you seriously when you explain how identity theft has destroyed company reputations and customer trust, diminished shareholder value, eaten away at market share. All of these things have resulted in business failures, personal fines and even jail time. If you can prove to asset owners that their systems are being compromised, you have a surefire business opportunity.

Take special note: If the client thinks the data on their network is not critical, there's no reason to call on him. Only clients who care about their data will spend money on infrastructure changes, application upgrades, performance improvements, and safeguards. But I'd counter with the following: "If a company has data that merits buying computers and networks, this client does have data worth protecting." The question, therefore, is: "Does the client understand the risks involved in failing to take the appropriate actions to secure his systems and data?"

The problem, once again, is ignorance. The foundation of your security value proposition is client education: teaching him what security is and why he's a likely target.

What About Your Clients?

How are other technology companies selling? Are they recommending security assessments? Probably. But are they more focused on compliance (Target was PCI compliant), general vulnerabilities, or are they thinking about the preemptive security strategies that must be in place before disaster strikes?

Imagine how big a hero the Home Depot sales rep would have been if he had only provided compelling justification. In Home Depot's case, it was actually the bank that figured it out! How embarrassing. But it's also a ding on those selling into the account. In Target's case they actually had technology in-house that would have detected the issue – they just weren't using it. Certainly there was a need…isn't that evident? And what would the ROI look like when compared to the millions of dollars these fiasco's are costing. Did they really have it covered, or was the sales team just ill-equipped to sell them on it? In Target's case the security analyst knew there was a need – why couldn't they get anyone's attention?

Chances are you have a client just like Target or Home Depot. Maybe not as big, but with a need just as important. It doesn't matter how big it is, cybercriminals are still interested. And the customers are still going encounter major life disruptions if their data gets stolen next week.

If you're waiting for senior management to approve some sort of budget, or finally see a need – don't hold your breath. They're busy. They're thinking about customer experience, more sales, and competitive pressures. The bigger companies are thinking about security, but chances are it's someone in IT who won't have a strong enough message to sell senior management on immediate action. Someone like the Target IT guy, waving his hand, but no one is listening.

CHAPTER NINE

Is Compliance Important?

> It is important, but not to you. Being compliant is far from being secure. When major corporations, deemed compliant, are successfully hacked, suddenly they are no longer compliant. How can that be?

In every security-sales class I conduct, I always ask, "Who has closed business in the last 12 months, with one of the federal regulations as the primary motivation for the client's decision to buy?"

In a class of 20 participants, I can count on there being one. Having taken this poll dozens of times over the last ten years, I'm confident technology sellers are not making quota off the wave of compliance growth. So, how important is compliance? How should technology companies approach compliance in the sales cycle?

Compliance is Important But Not To You

Target was compliant before they lost 40 million credit cards.

Heartland Payment Systems Inc., 7-Eleven Inc., and Hannaford Brothers Co. were all PCI compliant when Albert Gonzalez and his cohorts stole 130 million credit card numbers. Compliance has little to do with actually securing data.

I thought it was somewhat humorous that Hannaford was suddenly no longer considered compliant after being hacked. What exactly does that mean? Did something think being compliant meant no one would break it?

Any company can be hacked into. We've already established that. So what does compliance really mean? And "The scary thing is that once most businesses get the stamp of approval, that's sort of where they stay until they have a reason to investigate," says Steve Thomas, president of PwnedList. He's right.

Compliance and security, like most government programs have devolved into bureaucratic processes. A process designed to satisfy technically inept regulatory requirements that do little or nothing to protect critical business assets. What's worse is that many technology companies are capitalizing on this bureaucracy rather than providing effective security strategies for their clients. If you want to be the trusted advisor, you can't afford to be a bureaucrat. This is especially true with regards to the penetration testing industry as I'll discuss later in this book. The problem is, most asset owners don't really believe these threats are real.

Compliance requirements are difficult to understand. They are poorly defined, and generally satisfied with simplistic security products and paperwork. For example PCI requires anyone accepting credit cards to undergo regular penetration tests. Yet this requirement is undefined – what is a pen test? It could be anything. A simple external probe does it. But that really is a meaningless test. One news article likened this to testing bulletproof vests with a squirt gun.

Bots and hacking tools have become highly sophisticated weapons of mass destruction. We're no longer dealing with a simple virus here that threatens to erase your PC's hard drive. The actual attacks today are outpacing product and compliance laws. The perimeter can no longer defend the enterprise. Today's threats demand that companies start building what Mike McConnell, former Director of National Intelligence for the Federal U.S. Government, calls a "predictive edge". Companies need a perimeter that can "sense and preempt coming attacks, and if they do occur, to possess the tradecraft to immediately turn information and intelligence at the IT level into actionable, real-time insight for business leaders to respond to."

Accepting and understanding "that a remediation-centric cyber defense" won't do it, and that companies must work on communications between C-level executives, the board room, and IT, is critical to winning this war. **"Organizations need to change their entire security model from one of compliance – meeting basic standards for data protection – to a holistic multi-faceted program of engagement,"** writes McConnell, calling this the most important job of chief information security officers in 2014.

In other words, becoming a compliance expert isn't going to help your clients, so don't worry too much about learning the millions of laws out there that govern compliance.

Compliance is Still a Major Issue – Here's How You Benefit From It

Compliance is still a major issue and you can still use it in the sales process. Instead of working to become a compliance expert, learn enough to apply it. Great marketing happens when you meet people where they are, and take them to where they need to be. If they're working on compliance, you can use that awareness and momentum to begin the education process, leading them to a more secure computing environment.

The real value of compliance is that it has created a heightened awareness among corporate leaders. The growing number of new federal and industry regulations all seem to be focused on information theft and misuse, underscoring the growing threat against a company's digital assets. The bottom line: New laws are getting the attention of asset owners.

Compliance vs. Threats – How is the Sale Different?

There are several reasons a company buys security products. There may be a breach or incident, an impending threat, an upcoming or failed audit, or an initiative to become compliant. In each case, the sales cycle, buyer, and buying process will differ.

In the case of an incident or impending threat, the sales cycle is fast. They might not buy from you, but they have to do something. But as mentioned earlier, companies are not seeing the majority of today's surreptitious attacks. The number of opportunities stemming from actual attacks is far too small to consistently make quota – yet they're real and must be dealt with.

With compliance, sales cycles are longer. But in the polls I've conducted, neither compliance nor realized threats have driven many of the security deals sold by the average technology sales rep. The exceptions are small boutique companies that specialize in security or that focus on some aspect of compliance such as PCI audits.

Compliance is often approached by committee. Most regulations are farther-reaching than a network, server platform, or storage device. They involve business processes, personnel, training, and a host of considerations the technology sellers will never sell or consult on. The committee is frequently led by someone other than IT—perhaps a compliance officer, department head, CISO or other manager. Whoever leads the committee, it's not a formal hierarchy as we know it. As such, whatever decisions are made, they're not the choice of one person. This makes the sale more difficult. Addressing compliance head on—unless you work for a highly specialized consulting firm, is the wrong place to start.

Where Regulations Apply

Almost every company has some regulation with which it must comply. Some are industry regulations, such as Payment Card Industry Regulations (PCI), which apply to all companies storing credit card information.

HIPAA, while closely associated with medical organizations, may also apply to large corporations that store patient healthcare information—for example, part of an infirmary, fitness program, or employee assistance program. State and local government accounts also maintain HIPAA-regulated data (or patient healthcare information known in the industry as PHI.) For instance, in the school infirmary or a prisoner's health records. These are just a few examples to explore when consulting with clients.

Banks have thousands of regulations. It's not just GLBA. Banks are a complex web of bureaucratic red tape –some vertical knowledge is helpful before heading in to the EVP's office. So how to we make sense of all of this. There's too much for the average sales rep to get their arms around. In the next chapter I'll review some simple ways to work with compliance without getting your Ph.D.

CHAPTER TEN

Making Sense of Compliance

> The typical sales approach to compliance leads to long sales cycles and hours of meaningless meetings – Learn how to think about compliance and what your clients really need.

No One Is Actually Reading the Regulations

Unfortunately, reading the regulations proves to be a frustrating experience. Whether it's SOX, GLBA, HIPAA or another federal regulation, knowing enough to be an advisor in this space is out of reach for most. Manufacturers and resellers have been using lines like, "We can solve 'X' problem with 'Y' product" for years, but none of these products are actually mentioned in the regulations. The truth is, few people are actually reading these regulations, and few really understand what they mean.

That said, a new approach is needed—one that does not require the seller to memorize thousands of regulations. So instead of reading each regulation and putting in hours of research, let the client's committee perform this task. Let your clients' lawyers and department heads read and understand the data that must be managed under GLBA regulations, as well as where that data stays in the organization. Your job is to apply the appropriate security controls that deliver the level of security required by those who interpret the regulations.

But remember, this is not the same as delivering security. In fact, companies need to move away from compliance as a goal. Security is the goal, not compliance. To simplify the selling process and create a faster sales cycle, I believe there are three key principles that can be used to move from a compliance discuss back to security. Let's take a look.

Principle #1: Leveraging Due Care To Access Asset Owners

Where there are regulations and data, there is liability. Find the asset owner and understand his liability. Remember, IT doesn't really have any liability. Nor does the compliance officer.

Using the Concepts of Due Care

Due diligence and due care are two terms that are often confused in the disciplines of information security. I frequently hear them used interchangeably, but they are clearly different.

Due diligence can be thought of as an assessment process. Many regulations call for a proper assessment of some kind, so it's important to conduct one. But liability is not associated with assessment. In fact, an assessment's scope is not well defined and therefore cannot be easily targeted for noncompliance.

Due care, on the other hand, is associated with liability. The data owner must understand what it means to demonstrate due care in guarding corporate assets. The question is, did they take the reasonable steps necessary to secure data. **Put simply, due care involves using reasonable controls to protect data.** Per case law, if an incident lands companies in court, decisions regarding negligence in data treatment would be reviewed. The asset owner would be asked to prove he took reasonable steps to secure his data.

If the case involved a manufacturer of bricks, the court might ask an expert witness about minimal requirements. A simple firewall might be deemed adequate. However, if the manufacturer was involved in building weaponry for the U.S. military, reasonable steps would be far more stringent.

What About the Regulations?

I'm not a lawyer, so I urge salespeople to avoid addressing regulations directly. Let the compliance officer and legal do that. Instead, focus on due care.

Because regulations do not specify certain technology, moving toward due care is the safer way to go. In addition, regulations will change over time, as will threats. As your customers' security needs change, practicing due care and evaluating through due diligence will protect them from legal negligence.

In the coming chapters, I'll provide a simple way to look at security architecture to ensure due care is taken.

Principle #2: Differentiating With the ILM Framework

Once the asset owner understands due care, it's time to look more closely at their data.

Over the last twenty years, storage companies have made the concept of information life-cycle management (ILM) a popular way to sell storage. They've emphasized the need for different levels of availability, backup and recovery, cost per megabyte, and distinct performance levels from various media.

This concept, now well understood by executives, can be leveraged in the security sale. In fact, ILM is really a security issue. It speaks of the creation of digital assets, where they are used and stored, and where they're disposed of. This language puts the focus on the data rather than the infrastructure. This will be particularly important in the coming years as we see sales moving away from infrastructure, and more on software, data, and customer experience.

Since the data is what the company actually values, ILM can set you up for a much different discussion with asset owners. In the following section I describe six stages of ILM to show how data changes in value and risk over time:

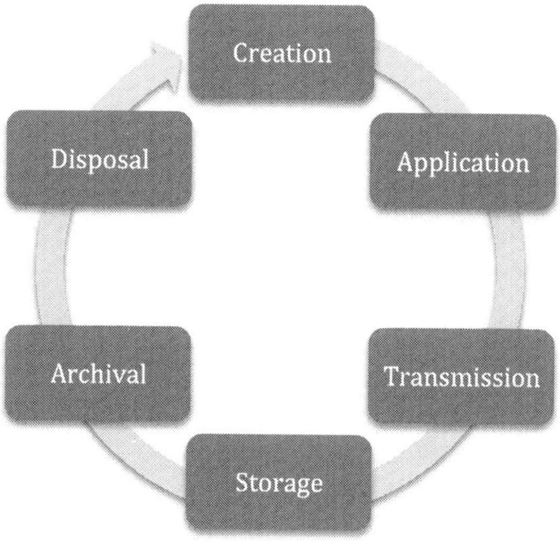

Creation: Each digital asset has a point of creation. This may be an email, Word document, database entry, or even a phone call or voice mail message left on a colleague's phone. This asset has a value, which the creator or asset owner must determine and categorize as confidential or public information, or something in-between. There are many levels of classification; rather than exploring each, it is safe to say the asset must somehow be classified and used according to policies that govern this type of data.

Application: Most assets are associated with an application. This may be order entry records, patient electronic medical records systems, or a project plan or design document in manufacturing. The asset owner or federal regulations may restrict access to this information by stating who may view, change, or delete it. The concepts of identity management come into play here to provide various users with providing authentication and levels of authorization to a given system. In today's world, this should be centrally managed using more than just passwords.

Transmission: We all understand networks. LAN, WAN, and wireless, as well as other forms of courier services, may be included in the transmission of data. The question is, what level of security is required when transmitting. It's a question more people should be asking before firing off a message at Starbucks.

Storage: While in use, data is stored. Most think their data is in the data center – it's not. Today our data is on laptops, smartphones, and on web facing applications. Data is everywhere. The trick is keeping up with data integrity and safeguarding it from unauthorized usage and theft. More and more our data will be in the cloud – a place no one can really see, but everyone can get to. Even when it's not their data.

Archival: Much of the data that comes from logs, communications involving financial reporting, and email are saved. Federal law and internal policies require it. This data is a little more challenging to deal with. For instance, email is data – but can your client get their hands on 5 year old email data if the court requests it? The likelihood is low, given the formats in which email is stored. Recovering data and maintaining its integrity require a good bit of forethought and perhaps specialized tools. Going forward, I expect to see more of this data in the cloud – a place that isn't as safe as we would like to think.

Disposal: The last stage of the data lifecycle process introduces some of the greatest risk and liability. It should be well thought out before it's time to delete these assets. While most end-users think deleting a file actually removes it, it doesn't. IT people may know this, you may know it, but the end-user is usually completely unaware of what data they are creating, holding, or exposing. So when an end-user sells their Smartphone, will there still be company data on it?

I recommend you memorize these stages. It's simple to remember them if you used the acronym CATSAD. With these six simple steps, you have a framework to ask executive-level questions, beginning with the creation of an asset.

Sample Questions might include:

- ☐ How sensitive is this data? Who is allowed to see it?
- ☐ Who has the authority to view it, change it, delete it or grant access to other users?
- ☐ Where are the applications that create or use it—and how secure are they?
- ☐ Where is this data transmitted? Is it used on wireless networks or sent through email over the Internet? Is it encrypted—or should it be? Are there various levels of security among the departments that create it or use it?
- ☐ How is it stored? How much data can you stand to lose? If your backups occurred last night and your system fails at the end of the next day, would you be able to recreate that data?

- ☐ How long does data need to be archived? If it is sent to offsite locations, should it be encrypted before leaving this facility?

- ☐ At what point is the information deleted? Do your policies state this, and are they enforced?

People Don't Understand Digital Assets

To secure data, it's critical to understand the difference between a physical asset, such as a chair or statue in the lobby, and the data companies rely on. These assets are intangible and invisible. It's digital, and it represents intellectual capital.

If a statue were stolen, you would see it one day and it would be gone the next. In the digital world data is kept in large systems behind locked doors. But as I've pointed out, it's not really in the data center. It can be stolen and still be there.

Bringing ILM Stages and Compliance Together

At each stage of ILM, security requirements change. Different threats exist, and appropriate controls are required. Looking at different ILM stages allows us to see what a regulation says about data each step of the way. Regulations will vary, but your job is not to interpret them. Instead, take your clients' interpretations of each stage and ensure technology exists to enforce policies. Once again, by using the concepts of ILM, you have an easy-to-remember framework for asking questions at the asset-owner level.

For example, when HIPAA data is created, we're talking about patient healthcare information (PHI). In the GLBA regulations, it's customer account information. Both regulations require only certain individuals to have access to the data on a need-to-know basis. This is an application issue. Both laws prohibit data from being transmitted in an insecure fashion—especially outside the organization, in an unencrypted manner. This may impact the use of wireless network access or email.

If you are a network provider, you are providing the secure transport of digital assets. The asset owner tells you which data is subject to the restrictions, where in the infrastructure it resides, who accesses it, etc. Once this is defined, your job as a solution provider is to deliver the capability to meet the asset owner's demands. You are not liable for failing to interpret the laws correctly, nor should you be.

Your goal at each stage of the ILM is to provide the client with the technology and best practices that comply with the concepts of due care. When this is properly done, regardless of pending regulations, your client should be covered.

Principle #3: The Power of Policy

Policy does two things. It drives architecture and limits liability. Most companies of a certain size seem to have a policy, but it often has little meaning to the organization.

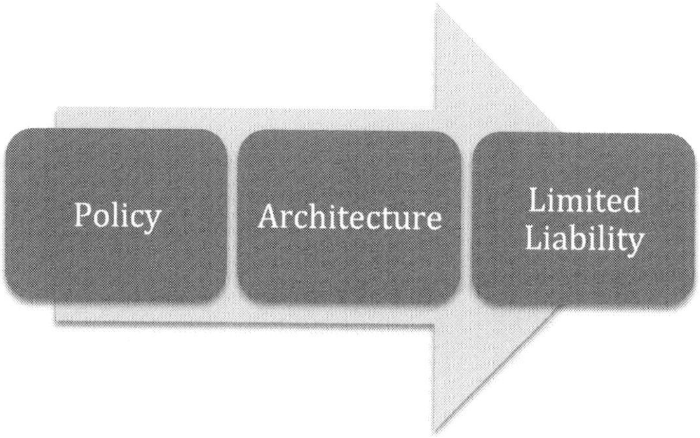

The power to limit liability lies in the enforcement and consistency of the policy. When a due-care issue arises or a violation occurs, the policy must be there to address it.

Compliance Is Driving Policy Changes

The link between policy and compliance is simple. As compliance areas are addressed, companies are changing policy. They must do this to limit liability. Policy drives architecture. It's critical that you, the seller, become involved in policy changes as they drive new architectural requirements.

For instance, I was working on a policy for a hospital. The company-specified technology standards called for certain products to secure the network's perimeter. But what if your company doesn't represent those products? Would another product do just as well? Policies and standards are not easily changed once senior management signs off on them. No one wants to have to reread and sign off another policy.

CHAPTER ELEVEN

Effective Boardroom Conversations

> Convince executives to rethink their security strategies – Get them asking, "Isn't it at least worth checking?" This begins the process of persuasion.

Back in the year 2000, I worked for a company that was acquired by a global integrator. After the transition, I began working to build a security practice for North America. It didn't take long to develop a business plan. The security market was growing, as were threats to the companies we solicited.

As a one-person security group, I wanted to work with our existing sales force to bring in midsize and large accounts. With my newly assigned quota in hand, I began calling salespeople nationwide to arrange meetings.

I was shocked, however, when the salespeople responded with hesitation. They didn't view security as a priority. But I wasn't about to give up.

I finally found a salesperson in South Carolina willing to hear me out. Now, if you're familiar with South Carolina, you know there aren't many large accounts there.

Regardless, he happily announced he had a small firewall upgrade opportunity. I wasn't thrilled at the prospect of a four-hour drive for a potentially small deal, but it was all I had.

My first concern was: "Are we meeting with an economic buyer?"

"Of course," the SC rep responded. "He's a vice president."

The prospect turned out to be a banker—and with three years of banking experience, I reminded the salesperson that virtually everyone who works at a bank is a vice president. To avoid a long drive, I recommended a phone consultation. The call ended with the salesperson agreeing to get a meeting higher up. Using a strategy I describe in detail in my book, *From Vendor to Adviser*, we soon had our meeting. So we set a date and I headed south.

I found myself seated in a meeting with three attendees from the customer side and the sales rep. The network administrator came to defend the bank's current firewall brand, the IT director, who was also the VP we were originally scheduled to meet with, was there to negotiate the deal, and the EVP put in an appearance, but really didn't understand why he was needed at this technical meeting.

How We Turned a Simple Firewall Lead Into A Year's Worth of Business

The executive has to be involved. But getting him there is not always that easy. In this chapter, we'll review the four key principles for communicating with executives and asset owners—the very principles, in fact, that made this sales call a success. I've used these concepts in many sales opportunities around the country and internationally. They work regardless of location or size.

Before going into the key points, let's examine the results of our meeting. First, we gained agreement to perform a large risk assessment instead of just quoting a firewall. But then look what happened. By approaching the assessment as a way to discover and justify more business, we came up with a year's worth of business including:

- ☐ Intrusion prevention appliances.
- ☐ Email security project.
- ☐ 24/7 security monitoring – managed services.
- ☐ An investigation into a potential hacking incident.
- ☐ Virtual private network sale (VPN).
- ☐ IP telephony implementation.
- ☐ And, of course, a firewall sale, with a failover configuration and maintenance.

In short, this meeting was a huge success. Let's explore how the sale was made. What can we learn from this, and how can we duplicate it? It's a process I've been using for over fifteen years and I still use it today, working with resellers through lunch & learn marketing events.

The Power of the Message

There's a disconnect in marketing. Great marketing is getting the right message to the right people at the right time. Every month resellers invite me to speak at lunch & learn meetings. And for ten years I have been averaging a 75% conversion rate. That means that on average 75% of the attendees are converting from sitting in seats to becoming clients of that hosting reseller. How is that possible?

The power is in the message. Every one of these attending companies has a security issue. We know that. But the hurdle is getting them to see it. First, we have to have the right audience. That means we're talking to asset owners. Second, we need a message that will compel them to move forward.

In my **Event Marketing Success Kit™** I provide seven important steps to achieving this. In this chapter I want to give you just one of these steps, the one that creates the conversion. It's the same process that I used in our South Carolina bank sales call.

The difference between the winning sales person and second place, is the message. You can only know so much about products and technology, and before the sale is made, it's hard for prospects to differentiate who the best provider is. The number one thing you can do to improve your position is to learn about marketing. When I say, learn about marketing, I am saying, learn how to move people forward with a compelling message. In my **Making Money w/ Security™** program, I spend the majority of the time on messaging and marketing strategy, not technology.

Most of the sales training I see out there is product focused. That's the last thing you need to be successful. I recently heard a sales trainer say, 80% of the product research has been done by the time prospects call you. Believe it. Google has replaced the presales engineer who focuses on product speeds and feeds.

In my book, *From Vendor to Adviser*, I cover a concept called the 5% rule. It simply says this; 5% of the potential buyers need what you are selling at any given time. They're out shopping. And they're looking for the best price. The other 95% might have the same need, and in the security space they really do. They just don't know it. Find the 95%, educate them, find a way to create justification, and you'll be ahead of every other competitor out there. This is key in selling security.

Know There's an Opportunity

Going into the bank meeting, I first needed to know an opportunity existed and where to find it. In the security arena, there's always an opportunity. That's an important mindset every sales rep should have. While this bank was shopping for a firewall, they had needs they didn't understand. That's where I took our conversation. I started with the firewall (starting our conversation right where they are.) But then, almost immediately took them to risk; showing them a greater need.

You've probably watched other sales teams try (or have tried yourself) to convince a buyer to invest in security by pointing to the countless news reports out there. This approach rarely works. After 15 years of security news, prospects have become numb to the realities of these reports. After all, what's the likelihood they'll discover they have been attacked on the week you meet with them, when there's no evidence of malicious behavior?

The next chapter will teach you what to say when you get to the asset owner level. I cover several strategies for getting to this meeting in my book *From Vendor to Adviser*, but once you get there, you'll need something to say. You'll need an effective message. One designed to convert your meeting into an opportunity to build a case for moving forward on projects, products, and managed services.

CHAPTER TWELVE

Know What Asset Owners Buy

> There are only four things you can sell an asset owner. If you're selling anything else, you're selling on price, and that means your margins are much lower than they should be – Your paycheck is the true test.

If you're going to convince buyers to move forward on security purchases or invest additional money on more secure infrastructure, you must prove their assets are at risk. You must show that the impact and likelihood of an incident justifies moving forward.

As explained in Chapter 1, buyers will spend money on only four things: return on investment (ROI), operational efficiency, competitive advantage and risk mitigation (security)—and security leads the list. Other sales books may label these priorities differently, but whatever nomenclature you use, it boils down to the same concepts. Here I'll provide a brief overview.

ROI (Return on Investment). In 1972, Mack Hanan wrote the popular book *Consultative Selling.* In his book he offers tremendous insights into using a database of norms to develop an ROI story. The problem with selling ROI in today's market however, is the number of unqualified people who have tried to make a case for ROI. Buyers have become leery of this argument, calling for empirical data and case studies many of us are ill-equipped to present. If you have a strong financial background, you may be able to pull it off, but the average salesperson breaks down when a CFO starts asking hard questions.

Operational efficiency can be a compelling argument. But when a 30-year-old stands in the office of a VP with 40 years of manufacturing experience, things can get rough. You may be asked: "And what do you know about management operations theory?" I list Operational Efficiency as the second best source of justification in *From Vendor to Adviser*, and for certain technologies and applications, it works very well. But it's not the easiest, and does require a fair amount of vertical expertise.

Competitive-advantage arguments pose the same problem when we're dealing with organizations whose industries are complex. Understanding vertical markets well enough to tell someone you're qualified to help him beat his competition takes courage and imagination. This argument works best with software and is probably the most effective software developer value proposition. But some serious research is required before going to the meeting.

Risk mitigation is altogether different. Here you're dealing with technology that changes all the time. Understanding risk is relatively easy for those well versed in technology. A systems or network salesperson can get up to speed on information security without years of experience – at least from the sales perspective. In almost every technology sale, I lead with security. It doesn't matter what I'm selling. Know the sound bites and you'll sound like an expert. Continue to study the sound bites and you'll be an expert. Case in point; I took the trends and sound bites commonly written about in the WSJ and published a book called, *Data@Risk*. When I show up at a lunch & learn to deliver my message, my audience sees me as the expert. You don't need years of hands on experience to do this.

In this chapter, we'll hit some of the basics on risk mitigation, then we'll turn our attention to marketing and messaging for the balance of the book. To be successful in the security business, you first need to know there really is an urgency out there. We've covered that. You then need some basics on security and risk, so we're covering that. Finally, you need to become an expert in marketing and messaging around risk. That's where we are headed.

Understand the Basic Principles of Risk Management

The ability to manage risk is what data owners really want. As those ultimately liable, they need to make sure company data is protected from misuse or theft. Remember, executives want to know the top five to seven major threats to their organization (said in business language,) what the odds are that they'll be hit (the impact vs. likelihood chart,) and whether they are trending up or down.

Their disinterest in meeting with you comes from too many sales people trying to sell hype and product. Don't be counted among one of the security "vendors" out there. Instead, transition your personal brand to that of risk advisor. Let's begin by looking at some security terminology.

AAA: To the average product salesperson, AAA is just another three-letter acronym, treated almost as though it's a word. To the executive, it may be an automobile club. But in the sales call, it provides a structure for some very important questions.

- ☐ **Authentication**: Identifying who's asking for data or network access—a critical area companies must control and maintain. Ask the data owner who should be accessing this information and how access is controlled.

- ☐ **Authorization**: Providing users with different levels of access privileges, including what they are allowed to see, change, create, delete, etc. Find out who provides different levels of authorization privileges. How is this controlled with the data in question?

- ☐ **Accountability**: The reporting mechanism that details who has access to specific information, who gave employees this access, when and what information was accessed, and what the employee did while accessing the data. Find out how this is done: Do they have a way to identify what users are doing?

MTD (Maximum Tolerable Downtime): A term often used in storage sales, but it's really a security question: How much downtime can you afford? The asset owner's answer likely differs from the custodian's. Find out how important data is and how long the company can survive if it's unavailable. This speaks to the impact of loss of availability. But ask the asset owner, not the custodian.

RPO (Restore Point Objective): Another storage term that focuses on how much data loss is acceptable. At what point must you be able to restore, and how much data can be lost between a backup and system failure? Again, this question focuses on the impact of data loss.

CIA (Confidentiality, Integrity, and Availability): Often considered the three pillars of security, each should be considered with the asset owner. Most of us think only of confidentiality or privacy of data, but the integrity and availability requirements are equally important.

Attack Surface: This deals with the number of technologies, applications, and access points accessible from the outside. For instance, how many websites, mobile apps, and web pages does your prospect have, and how do they keep track of what's theirs and what might be rogue?

Actionable Intelligence: Is your prospect collecting and analyzing events. The ability to proactively see what happening, who might be attacking, and the ability to detect and respond early is the next step in defending the enterprise.

Each of these topics is used to build a picture of risk in the mind of the buyer. Risk is simply a look at impact versus likelihood.

The concepts above provide a framework for asking questions that uncover key assets, as well as the impact associated with losing confidentiality, availability, data integrity, etc. If the impact is high, the issue is worth considering. The question is, what is the likelihood?

When a plane goes down, the impact is always high. The question risk managers start asking center around the likelihood of this happening again. What is the likelihood that a plane will be sitting on a runway that's too short, while air traffic control is staffed by only one person who's not paying attention and gives the go-ahead to take off? The pilots, unfamiliar with the airport, push their throttles forward and accelerate down the runway, only to find the strip is too short. You may remember an incident like this from 2006. A major tragedy resulted. So, what is the likelihood it will happen again? Is it high enough for someone to do something about it?

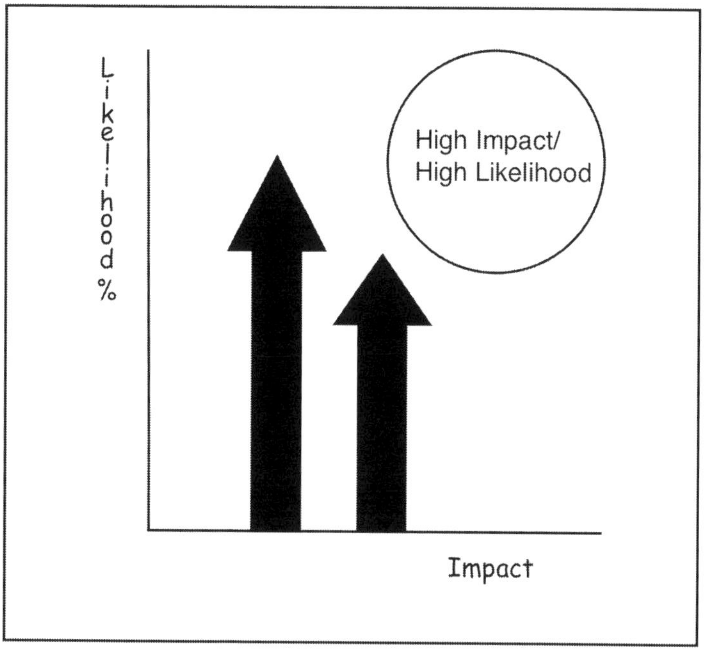

Figure: Justification For Change

As a salesperson, you have little ability to change impact; however, you can change likelihood. Your sales call should focus on likelihood, looking for the safeguards that may be used to reduce the likelihood of data being compromised. Later I'll come back to managed services, but here I'd like to point out that managed services should almost always be sold as a way of maintaining an acceptable level of risk. Once the risk level has been brought back into an acceptable range through remediation efforts – someone has to maintain it. This avoids the price pressures most managed services providers are under.

Layers of Security

When selling a security strategy, the concept of security layers working together to protect assets allows you to create a vision. As you will see in later chapters, it doesn't make sense to sell a security product by itself, unless you're simply completing another provider's security strategy. Three types of controls must be considered:

Technical controls: Traditional security controls like firewalls, intrusion detection software, access control, etc. Most companies will at least have a firewall in place and perhaps VPN technology. More are implementing intrusion detection/protection software and appliances, but they alone will not protect data.

Physical controls: Examples of these controls include controlled access to wiring closets/datacenters. Security cameras or even security guards may be positioned in the lobby. Your client will frequently have some form of protection, but will often lack proper security in public-access locations. This is especially true with mobile devices. In most cases a smartphone is completely open as far as physical security goes. If someone can physically steal it, it's not well protected.

Administrative controls: These are almost always inadequate. Security policies, disaster recovery, business continuity plans, and security and event correlation reports fall into this category. Companies usually lack well-written policies.

Four Big Problems That Will Derail Your Sale

Now, here is the problem when it comes to selling security. Actually there are four.

The Sales Problem. The sale is technical – too technical. Sales calls focus on technical people, technical products, and are conducted using technical presentations. The smarter your presales technical guy is, the better you feel about your chances of winning. On the other hand, there's no pressing need and the deal often comes down to price comparisons.

The Marketing Problem. Earlier I referred to the marketing disconnect. Most sales people are not happy with their marketing department. And marketing is not happy with you. If you're a marketing professional with real marketing expertise, or you have one in your company, you're one of the few. Most of the resellers, and even smaller manufacturing companies don't have marketing people who understand direct response marketing. Big companies spend millions on branding, but that doesn't translate into sales in your region.

The Assessment Problem. With compliance laws and uncertainty, people are assessing security. However, the assessments are not turning into remediation projects. I like to say, "They are not converting." Only about 20% of the assessments I see turn into projects or managed services contracts. Given that almost all assessments turn up issues I would call "Urgent", it doesn't make sense that they wouldn't convert to project work almost every time. Most assessments are too technical, focus on the wrong things, don't highlight the urgency, and never reach the asset owner.

The Presentation Problem. Chances are your company presentation is boring. It looks like every other technology-company presentation. It starts with your company name, how big you are, years in business, certifications, some great clients, and the products or services you provide. They all look the same. If you've had trouble booking new appointments to show your corporate presentation, I'm not surprised.

Fixing the Four Basic Problems

Almost every company I run into has these same problems. But there are solutions. Security is going to be central to solving these problems.

Fixing the Sales Problem.

Every leader surrounds themselves with advisors. The President of the United States is a great example. Whether you believe what Obama (our current president) says or not, his written speeches are well done. Especially the early speeches that got him elected. Are you sitting down? He didn't write them himself. But he's not the only one. Corporate leaders often have others advising them on just about everything, especially when it comes to stuff they don't understand.

Leaders may have health advisors (doctors, trainers, and more), sports advisors (out on the golf course), financial advisors (investments, tax strategies, realtors, etc.). They might have marriage advisors, teenager advisors (counselors), religious advisors, and life advisors (life coaches.) Who is advising them on information security? They won't look to IT for it. Remember Mike McConnell's comment cited earlier, about bringing down the wall between IT and the executive team? It's needed, but it's not happening. These people need an advisor.

The question is, how do you become that trusted advisor? It starts with the sound bites. The trusted advisor is trusted and able to advise. Be honest, and maintain a reputation that is above reproach. But you're also going to have to develop that ability to advise in the area of risk management. Learn the sound bites and know the trends. Spend just a few minutes each day and you'll get their. You should also be learning about the businesses your call on and reading the books these business leaders are reading. Spend less time on email and data sheets. Spend more time studying the people you call on and the things that would concern them if they knew about them.

Fixing the Marketing Problem

Security is predictably broken in just about every company. Marketing, as I stated earlier, is getting the right message to the right people at the right time. People with liability need that urgent message right now. But it's got to be delivered in a way they can receive it. There also has to be a direct response component.

Recall some of the earlier security concepts such as CIA. Learn what assets (data) must be kept confidential, where integrity is of utmost importance, and what must be available for a company to remain viable. What is predictably in trouble in the companies you are calling on? Is their disaster recovery program well planned and tested? Almost never. Malware is almost always present – where is it and how does it potentially threaten the organization? You can't possibly know all of this without an assessment, but it's predictable even before conducting one.

Stop delivering your generic company overview. Don't expect them to come up with projects they are willing to hand over. Instead, start marketing to predictable needs. Regardless of what your company is promoting right now, you can build a brand around your specialization (one of the four areas mentioned above,) and you can begin your own direct response marketing program right now.

If you're a reseller, chances are you can do a lot of marketing with channel development money. The **Event Marketing Success Kit™** is just one example of direct response marketing. Your company probably already does these events, but are they converting to business? If you were to invest in just one marketing program, learning to convert large groups through lunch & learns would be it. Turn a laborious activity, that you're already involved in, into a major source of income.

By direct response, I mean you are not branding or just sending out data sheets. Direct response is the only kind of marketing that really matters when it comes to your sales efforts. The offer will be urgent, providing the prospect with information that will show them they have a need. Your message will be clear, followed by a clear call to action. Here, my goal is to give you the same security message I have successfully used for years to make that conversion happen.

Back in chapter one I talked about Randy's transition from selling PCs to specializing in security. Randy was afraid he would be limiting his sales by focusing on security. But in reality, his business only prospered. Why? By specializing, Randy's company became branded as experts in the area of security for small businesses in his area. Notice he did not spend his marketing dollars on rebranding. Rather, he spent it on direct response marketing. He was laser focused on SMB security, targeting business owners. It was direct response in that his company presented clear urgent messaging to asset owners, with a clear call to action. And by doing this, his company was naturally rebranded without the big expense of rebranding exercises. In this chapter I will show you the exact message we used to move his audience of business owners, who didn't really know they had a need, from sitting to buying.

Fixing the Assessment Problem

In my **Making Money w/ Security™** workshop, one of my favorite exercises is reviewing actual assessment deliverables submitted by my attendees. This is one of the most eye-opening exercises. Having looked at hundreds of assessments from all over the world, I've been amazed to find that they all look the same.

It's probably because everyone copies the next guy. Companies continue to look at what their competition does, and then copy it without measuring the response. Part of direct response marketing is measuring conversion rates. When a company sends out an ad with a tear out card, they track that card to see what the response rate is. The assessment document is no different. It must be tracked. Stop looking at your competition and start measuring your conversion. If an assessment deliverable isn't converting 70% - 90% of the time, it's time for a change. I'll cover this in more detail shortly.

Fixing the Presentation Problem

We'll spend the rest of this chapter on great presentations. Like the assessment, if the presentation isn't converting, it's not working. Presentations are direct response marketing activities. Whether your presenting assessment findings or a company overview, you're there to convert that audience to the next thing. It might be an initial sale, or it might be the next step in remediation. It should be tracked, analyzed, and tweaked for optimal conversion.

Ten years ago when I started Stelzl Visionary Learning Concepts, Inc., I started primarily as a speaker. The first thing I did to really learn about the industry was join the National Speakers Association. The one thing that impresses me most about a great speaker is their ability to move an audience to action. Whether it is a health and wellness keynote, motivational speech, or sales expert, a great speaker will have an audience of hundreds or thousands taking action in just 60 minutes! Can a sales person do the same thing? The answer is yes. In fact, I have an entire workshop devoted to this one life changing topic, ***Mastering Board Room Presentations™***. Presentation skills or public speaking is one skill every sales person would be wise to invest in.

Five Things I've Learned From High-Priced Consultants

Fixing these four problems should be a top priority. Before we go on to talk about presentation, there are five things I mention in my book, *From Vendor to Adviser*, that bear repeating:

Assessments are marketing tools. When you conduct an assessment and find issues, it's your job to convert that client from assessment to remediation. If a doctor knows his patient has cancer, and fails to convert them to some type of treatment plan, he's failed. His patient may die as a result. He should be asking, "How can I communicate this message in a way that moves my patient to action before it's too late?"

Advisors develop road maps. Advisors don't sell point products. Instead, they analyze where a company is today, where it needs to go, and how to get there. They then get paid incredible sums of money to move that client from point A to point B.

Sell results, not methods. No one is interested in your methodology or product. The asset owner is trying to build a business that requires greater efficiencies, competitive advantage, and safeguards that keep them from derailing. Focus on the outcomes necessary to move your client forward, not the components that are used to build the solution.

Fees are commensurate with value. Again, this is a topic I spend a entire chapter on in *From Vendor to Adviser*. Security work can be some of the highest paid services work in the IT industry. Learn to value price – this one thing will completely change your personal income – for the better.

Presentation is everything. The deal is sold through the presentation, not the brochure, or the proposal, or your website. It doesn't matter whether it's on a Google+ Hangout, Skype call, phone call, lunch & learn, or live one-on-one meeting, great sales people are great presenters. This is one skill every sales person should be working to master. Learn to master the board room presentation.

Gaining Permission With Asset Owners

Earlier I mentioned that 75% of the executive level or business owner attendees at our lunch & learns sign up or take action in the form of an assessment. How is that possible? In the next chapter I want to show you a presentation I started using fifteen years ago to sell security solutions. I still use it today and it still gets the same response. This year, this one presentation as converted over 90% of the lunch & learn attendees I've spoken to.

"You get delegated to those you sound like," writes Michael Bosworth. Remember this quote every time you walk into a decision maker's office. Then, when you're redirected to the IT group, admit you must have sounded like an IT person: way too technical. If you're going to sell security, you need a message that hits the asset owners where they are now, and takes them where they need to go.

Earlier I mentioned the regional bank in South Carolina. I used the presentation I'm getting ready to show you to make that sale. As I drove down to Charleston S.C. that day, I had a decision to make: How do I keep the meeting focused on the asset owner? With the technical person and decision maker both in the room, we somehow needed to keep the meeting interesting to that executive. Once a technical line of discussion begins to dominate, the executive leaves—something we've all experienced. But it's not exactly the presentation that creates the conversion. It's the principles behind the presentation that make it all work. So as you go through this next chapter, pay attention to two things. First, the presentation and how it flows. But secondly, and more importantly, study the marketing principles and begin to apply them to all of the presentations and meetings you are responsible for.

CHAPTER THIRTEEN

The House, The Cloud & The Coverage Model

> A simple way to grab the attention of asset owners. You need permission to build justification; This is how you'll get It.

(Note: There is an excellent live recording of this presentation on my Private Membership Site. At the end of this book I'll show you how you can get that recording for FREE.)

The Message That Has Consistently Converted 75% of The Audiences I Speak To

I call it **The House, The Cloud, and the Coverage Model™** (which I will refer to as, The House & the Cloud for the remainder of the book.) It all begins with what I call, "The Three Big Questions." It's a simple presentation designed to show asset owners exactly how security works, and points out the one major mistake being made by 90% of the companies out there. When they see this, they just about always begin to question their own company's approach.

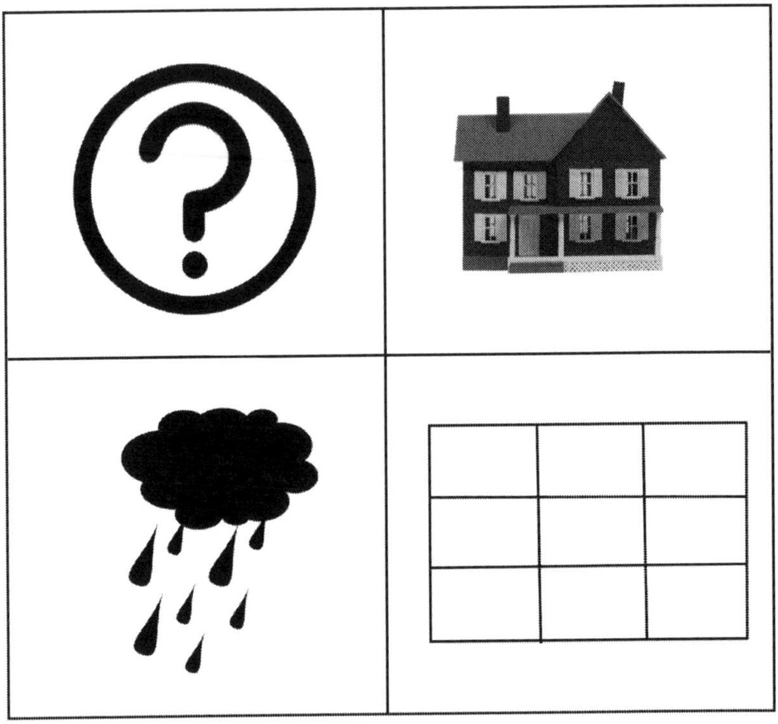

Figure: The Framework

When I present The House & the Cloud, my goal is simply to get permission to find the urgent issues in my client's computing environment. Before they hear this, security is one of those things that just seems out of reach. It's under the direction of the IT group or compliance so it's taken care of. When I finish, they suddenly understand how it works. They see how easily they can be compromised. By following a few guidelines they can fix 80% of the problem – all in a nontechnical way. This almost always leads to an opportunity.

From the diagram above, the framework works like this:

- ☐ Three Questions
- ☐ The House
- ☐ The Cloud
- ☐ The Coverage Model

Step 1: Turn the Meeting From Products to a Risk Discussion Using Three Simple Questions

When selling security you must have access to asset owners. Asset owners have liability. But what are you going to talk about if you can't discuss products? In every sales call, I use the same outline. I start with the three questions, modifying them based on the situation. The S.C. bank meeting was no exception. Turning to the buyer, I asked these three questions:

- ☐ **Question 1:** What are you trying to protect?
- ☐ **Question 2:** What are the relevant threats?
- ☐ **Question 3:** How comfortable are you with your organization's ability to detect and respond to a recognized threat before data is compromised?

Question 1 – What are you trying to protect?

Your first objective: Steer away from a product meeting and focus on assets. The first question takes you right to your prospect's mission-critical data, simply asking him to identify it.

Again, the person you must speak with is the asset owner – they are the only ones who can answer this question. You're not looking for the security administrator's opinion. You want to know the asset owner's position on what really matters.

There are a number of acceptable answers, but "the network" isn't one of them. You're looking for data that exposes the owner to liability or places the company's reputation in jeopardy. When I ask this question, I explain I'm looking for the items that would greatly impact the business if compromised or inaccessible. If the question is framed correctly, I expect dialogue on mission-critical systems. In my S.C. meeting, we spent the first 20 minutes of our meeting on this first question. At the end of our dialogue, I had a thorough understanding of the client's key assets and the impact associated with loss or compromise.

Marketing Principle. Notice, this is not just an aimless Q&A session. Matthew Dixon, in *The Challenger Sale*, makes it clear that executives don't have time for open ended sales questions. My question predictably gives me the X-Axis of the impact vs. likelihood graph.

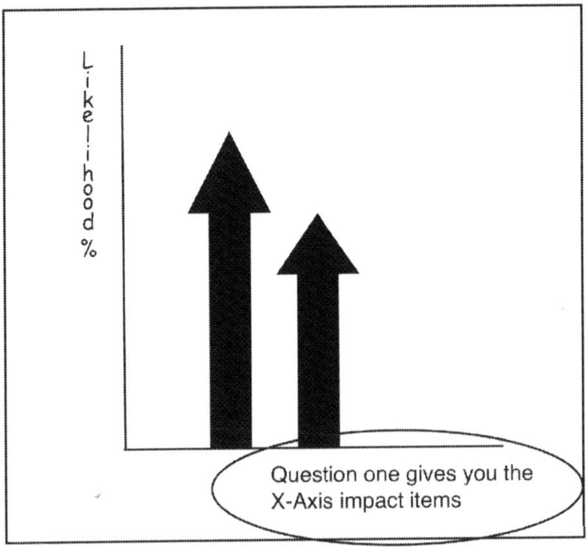

Figure: Using Question One

Question 2 – What are the relevant threats?

Next, I must determine the likely threats. The data owner may not be aware of all his impending security threats. Finding out what he believes is real—and most risky to his company—is helpful in developing a business case for security.

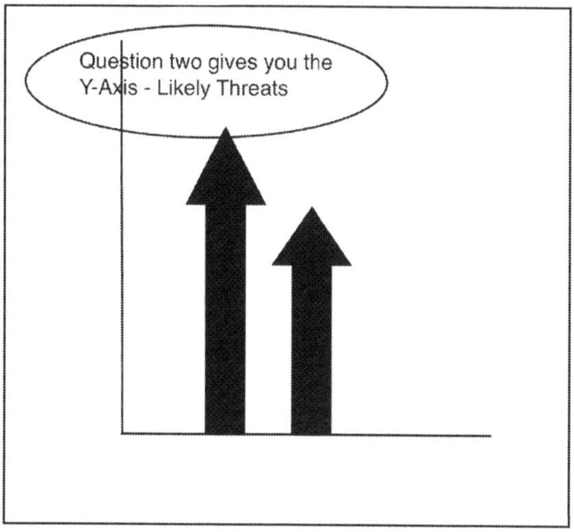

Figure: Using Question Two

Risk levels depend a lot on business conditions. For instance, if the company is involved in a legal battle, risk levels will be affected. What if he's laying off IT people, has challenges with other internal staff, uses various contractors, or is open to other guest users. This is a good time to uncover any past security issues. In my S.C. meeting, we spent another 10–15 minutes on this topic.

Marketing Principle. Notice here that while I am continuing to gather specific information, I am really building my impact vs. likelihood graph. By asking question two, I now have a clear understanding of the likely threats from the buyer's perspective. I have part of the Y axis on the risk graph.

Question 3 – How comfortable are you with your ability to detect and respond before it's too late?

The final question is a quick one. Determining the prospect's comfort level with his current security strategy will tell you a great deal about how well he understands today's security threats. In most cases I hear clients saying, "I don't know, " or looking to their IT person for an answer. Don't let IT answer. Politely tell them you are not looking for technical information at this point. You need the asset owner to either admit he doesn't know, or make a statement about where he sees his own level of asset protection. This will give you what we need to carry on the meeting.

Marketing Principle: Question three completes the risk graph, providing a picture of how likely the asset owner believes these threats may be.

If, for example, your prospect is very comfortable, you know you have to do some educating. If they agree the risk is high, you'll want to reinforce that belief by showing them why that is. Given all that we've covered so far, it's hard to believe anyone would feel "very" comfortable with their security.

By the time you've asked the third question, you should have a clear understanding of your buyer's key assets, top threats (the ones they know about), priority of systems, and comfort level. You have the entire risk graph built – from their perspective.

At this point, you must provide a compelling reason to consider changes in the organization's approach to security. You haven't sold anything at this point, and your goal is not to argue a case. It's simply to understand what their perception is of the impact vs. likelihood graph. And then to gain permission to investigate their current level of risk – to build the real impact vs. likelihood graph.

Let me reiterate: These three questions are designed to shift the focus from products to assets. Technical security influencers then no longer need to defend their current product choices. I asked these three questions while sitting at the table in S.C., doing more listening than talking. My primary goal was to understand how the asset owner sees his own security before launching into my presentation.

> The purpose of the three questions: Stop focusing on product, and focus on assets—what are you trying to protect.

Step 2: The House – Positions You As The Advisor

The three questions will consume most of your meeting time. They allow you to build the risk graph, providing a clear picture of where the opportunity exists. Your next goal is to reposition yourself as their risk advisor.

The House is a simple analogy designed to quickly show the client they really don't understand security, but you do. You'll start this discussion by showing your prospect how any security architecture must operate if it is to be effective. You want them to see that most companies, including theirs, have likely approached security incorrectly. I use the analogy of a house: a physical structure we all think of as a safe place to be.

As I walk through this presentation, I'll provide marketing tips along the way explaining why this model works. You don't have to use this exact presentation for the security sale to work, but you do have to follow the principles if you want to succeed.

In my S.C meeting, after asking the three questions, I stood up and went to the whiteboard. As I went, I asked, "**Have you ever thought about how security works? Have you ever considered what actually makes something secure? I mean, all security – whether a bank, a house, or even a prison?**"

At this point I drew a simple house on the whiteboard, and

asked the buyer to share how he secures his house. During this brainstorming exercise, my prospect began listing typical home security measures. “Doors,” “windows,” “locks,” “gun,” “dog,” “alarm,” etc. From his answers I created a simple chart on the white board that looked something like this:

Doors	Alarm	Dog
Locks	Motion detector	Gun
Windows	Monitoring	Police
Fence	Crime watch	Insurance

Purposely, I have listed all 12 components in three columns; that will become clear in a moment. Having done this presentation hundreds of times, there are 12 items that always come out. They might use slightly different words, but in general, these 12 work. I recommend you memorize this list.

From the list, our discussion went something like this:

“These are the components most of us look to, to protect our homes and loved ones. However this is not actually what is protecting us.”

“It’s actually a system that is at work here.”

I then divide this list into three columns, asking the buyer to help me categorize his lists. Notice that I’ve grouped the items in a particular order, regardless of how they were given to me.

1.	2.	3.
Doors	Alarm	Dog
Locks	Motion detector	Gun
Windows	Monitoring	Police
Fence	Crime watch	Insurance

"What three categories are represented here?"

Businesspeople usually guess that the first list applies to a home's physical features; however, they are all physical. I refer to Column 1 as my **proactive protection column**. Once Column 1 is labeled, the second column is obvious. It's about detection. Column 3 applies to response. **It's my PDR Model: protection, detection, response. Every security architecture in the world (that works) is based on these three pillars.**

It's now time to ask an important question: "Which column is most critical to security?"

Most asset owners choose Column 1: protection. They believe keeping things out is always best. While this is theoretically true, security architecture has always relied more on Column 2 to secure assets. Every time my prospect answers incorrectly, and I can show him why in a simple, credible answer, it puts me further into the advisory role.

At this point I explained why DETECTION is the primary focus. We were sitting in a bank, and I asked my client if his doors were open. He replied yes. I then asked if his vault was open; again, he responded with a nod.

"So, what is protecting the money?" I asked. There are many

layers of security in a bank. Cameras and security guards observe activity throughout the day. If someone violates a policy, steps behind the teller line, draws a weapon, or wanders down the wrong hallway, a well-timed response plan will kick in. And how about at night? The doors are locked, but could easily be broken through if crooks don't care about the threat of the alarm system.

One's house, too, has no real security without detection. The idea that your doors or windows will deter a determined intruder is clearly wrong thinking.

Again, the point of these comparisons is to draw our buyer into a clear example he's very familiar with—to show him there are three critical aspects to security architecture and that the detection process is vital to asset protection. With a few quick and familiar analogies, he was convinced.

Marketing Principles of the House

Throughout this presentation I am working on getting the right message to the right person at the right time. But the right message has to connect with that person. It has to grab their attention and pull them into the storyline.

There are five key aspects of an effective marketing message as discussed in Chip and Dan Heath's book, *Made to Stick*, and all five are used here:

- ☐ **Simple** – the message has to be easy to understand.
- ☐ **Concrete** – the listener must be able to visualize the concepts being presented.
- ☐ **Disruptive** – The content must disrupt their thinking, causing them to see new insights.
- ☐ **Credible** – The message, with it's new content must be believable and compelling.

- ☐ **Emotional** – The message must be emotionally impactful if it is to move them to action.

There are four more key principles for effective teaching. They involve:

- ☐ **Knowledge gaps** – creating questions in the mind of the listener, that demand an answer. This keeps them tuned in as I present.
- ☐ **Interruptions** – every few minutes there must be something that jolts them awake; that causes them to question the path they are currently on.
- ☐ **Commitments** – most listeners think they already know what you're going to tell them. By forcing them to provide answers, to commit to a vote on something, I have the opportunity to prove to them that they don't really understand the complex issues I am presenting.
- ☐ **Unexpected revelations** – every presentation or teaching session must bring the learner to knew levels of understanding. Listeners must leave this meeting having gained new and useful knowledge.

When a speaker applies these concepts, the audience moves. Here's what I just did with the House.

I started with a KNOWLEDGE GAP. Getting up from the table I said, "Let me show you how security works." I positioned myself as the advisor by claiming to be the authority, and then demonstrated it by getting them to commit to the security model used to secure their home. I then showed them a model they had not considered, and asked them to comment on the most important factors. The more wrong choices they make, the better off I am; as long as I can come up with credible explanations, such as the banking example, to show that I am right. Each time I am moving closer to becoming their advisor.

It's important that this be presented carefully and with humility. I'm definitely taking a "Challenger" position (See *The Challenger Sale, Taking Control of the Customer Conversation*, by Mathew Dixon and Brent Adamson.) I want to be careful to let them down slowly. Along the way I let them know that most people think the way they do, because that is how we've been taught the think. But it's wrong thinking. I go into great detail on this process in my ***Security Sales Mastery Program™***.

Step 3: Show How Easy it is To Break in

Once the buyer sees that detection is the most important area to focus on, it's now time to illustrate how easily one can infiltrate a company's network. I like to draw a simple two-cloud network, showing the internal network and the Internet; then, I quickly demonstrate how a bot network (botnet) is established.

There are many roads into a network, including email, instant messaging (IM), phone app downloads, and compromised websites. The most basic music, video and picture downloads can be used to infect systems.

Certainly more than half of the spam out there is infected. If I were an attacker, all I would need to do is convince the recipient to click on a link or open a file, allowing me to install malware on their system. And all I need for access is one computer out of the hundreds or thousands a company might own. In our threat chapter, we reviewed how this is done, so without providing all of the technical details, I illustrate how I can bypass firewalls and take over. The point is, firewalls don't stop many of the threats used by organized crime in this information-theft era.

> **Key Principle: It's easy to break in - anyone who really wants to can and will.**

As I go through the model, I list several important sound bites. For instance:

- ☐ 250,000 systems are infected by bots every day.
- ☐ 75% of end-users admit that they steal company data.
- ☐ 35% of Android devices were exposed during the Heartbleed bug.
- ☐ Every major company in the U.S. has been successfully hacked into.
- ☐ The U.S. DoD has told us, they can no longer keep perpetrators out. They can only manage what's accessed.

- ☐ NASA spent $58 million on security last year and they were still hacked.

It's after these alarming (WSJ) sound bites that I present the key question—the point where I exposed my prospect's weaknesses. Turning back to the house model, I asked him: "Which column does your company rely on most to protect your digital assets?"

The answer is predictable. The company may have some intrusion prevention software running at the perimeter, but the ability to detect and respond to attacks throughout the computing environment is generally quite weak. Most of your customers will be unable to detect and respond to attacks coming from wireless networks, remote access, compromised laptops, Bluetooth technology, and personally owned and managed computing devices.

When this process is handled correctly, the data owner will realize his security strategy was built around an approach that sounded good 20 years ago: the idea that a firewall would protect the internal network from Internet threats and that a password would do the rest. At this point, without debating with the technical team, you've brought your buyer to a new level of understanding.

Marketing Principle

The cloud is a simple transition from a physical, concrete example, to something less understandable by the business executive. In my diagram, I steer clear of complex network drawings, and at all costs avoid taking input from the IT team on what their network actually looks like.

In this section of my presentation I am using alarming sound bites that are credible, because they are based on the WSJ sound bites I've been collecting. I only spend a few minutes on the bot, to show them a concrete illustration of how the hacker works. The rest is sound bites.

Remember, the IT people can't argue with you as long as you are just quoting from the WSJ. When you use far reaching numbers and statistics, you gain more credibility, which strengthens your position as the advisor. The IT person has not read the WSJ, so they won't be able to comment. The key here is to have enough sound bites memorized, along with the source and date, to show that you know what you're talking about.

When you ask them which column they mostly rely on, you create another knowledge gap. They probably don't really know the answer, but by leading the question with – "Do you tend to use firewalls and passwords, or do you know what everyone is doing at any given moment?" they usually see that the latter is not likely true in their company. Larger organizations may actually have this type of monitoring technology in place, but most companies don't.

Note here that the sound bites are not emotional, and therefore actually slow down the sales process. However this step is necessary as it establishes your credibility, defeats any push back that may come from IT, and allows the buyer to see where their problem is.

You may ask at this point, "What if the buyer doesn't agree"? Take him back to Column 1 of the house model. What would you have to do to secure the house through Column 1? Some military facilities rely heavily on Column 1, yet those in charge understand it's not enough. With a house, you'd need to spend hundreds of thousands of dollars—and even into the millions—to create a perfectly safe home without relying on detection schemes. And still it wouldn't really work. Does the buyer really want to build a castle with insurmountable walls, moats and razor wire? It's completely "over the top" and unnecessary when you realize it costs about $30 a month to hire a security monitoring company, with alarm equipment included. It becomes clear, with proper analysis, that detection response is a key part of any security strategy—and your prospect's security architecture likely lacks this type of approach.

Step 4:– Closing the Gap With Holistic Security

Explaining the holistic security approach is the final step in your meeting. I call this table "The Coverage Model." It gives the data owner a better understanding of how the right security will defend corporate assets. But it also closes the final knowledge gap. At the end of Step 3, I ask the buyer how they protect their data. At that point they either don't know, or don't realize they are using column one. Either way, they need some answers. The gap stands; how can they get from where they are to where they need to be? This is the job of the high-priced consultant. This is no longer a point product deal.

	P	D	R
Admin	Policy		BCP/DR
Tech		IDS	
Physical		Checking badges	Guards

Taking the concepts from the house illustration—protection, detection and response—and combining them with three basic types of security controls (administrative, technical, and physical) I can then construct a simple coverage model. Don't fill in the entire table; instead, quickly illustrate how these nine boxes provide a comprehensive approach to securing data. Most companies focus on these boxes as silos or spend the majority of their time working on just one or two areas. Data owners really need to view these as integrated controls that work together through the infrastructure and organization to enable a strong security architecture.

Now back to my S.C. bank sales call. Using this diagram, I looked at the decision maker and said: "It's not the firewall we should be talking about. As you can see, these issues have little to do with firewalls and brute-force hacking." Security is not a firewall conversation; it's a matter of assets and risk, the likely threats and their ultimate impact.

The buyer may, at this point, ask whether security will prevent hackers from breaking in and stealing his data. My response: "No, I guarantee they will break in. The question is, will you be able to detect and respond before your assets are compromised?"

Bringing These Four Principles Together

Now, I am not suggesting that you draw this house in every sales call; however, the house works. People have said, "I don't think I could draw that simple picture for a CIO of a major corporation." Well, I have. I have used it in board meetings, executive-level association meetings, keynotes, sales calls, informal dinners, and dozens of lunch and learns where over 75% have consistently signed up for an assessment.

My audience generally responds, "You are the first person who has been able to explain this complex topic in terms I can really understand."

But it's not the house that matters; it's the key principles:

- ☐ **The three questions**: move the meeting away from product and onto the assets. You can do this any way you want, but somehow you must set the foundation for the meeting at the executive level—and on the assets.

- ☐ **The House**: However you want to do it, you must show the buyer what security really is and get him to admit he doesn't have it. Protection, DETECTION, response, seems to work well.

- ☐ **The Cloud**: Asset owners need to see how easy it is to break in and that the firewall team doesn't really understand this. It's not a firewall issue anymore.

- ☐ **The Coverage Model**: Finally, they need to see that this is not a product issue that should be delegated to the IT organization. Asset protection requires holistic thinking around products, policies, procedures, education, etc. It's a big issue, and they need someone who really understands it to guide them down the right pathway.

Security Sinkholes

In my security-sales workshops, attendees frequently ask, "What if prospects have everything they need—or say they have it all covered?" It's a great question—and it will happen.

First, if you're talking to a data owner or other senior manager, he generally won't assert he has everything covered. The most common response tends to be: "I don't know." At that point they'll turn to their IT person looking for some answers.

For the company that has done everything reasonable to secure its data, I whip out my trusty security sinkhole list—a compilation of the areas almost always lacking in due care:

- ☐ Compliance

- ☐ Policy and liability

- ☐ Wireless

- ☐ Centralized identity management
- ☐ Remote access
- ☐ Applications such as websites used by your clients
- ☐ BCP/DR
- ☐ Messaging and email
- ☐ Mobility/BYOD
- ☐ Collaboration applications such as Google+
- ☐ Unauthorized cloud applications
- ☐ The "People Factor"

In particular, areas like BYOD (and any mobile end-point,) collaboration, cloud, user awareness, and web application security are severely lacking. The perimeter may have most of what's needed, but when we start moving to these other areas, I find networks and systems to be very insecure. With this in mind, I remind the asset owner that every major organization has been successfully hacked according to the U.S. department of defense (WSJ Sound Bite), exposing millions of people and corporate/government secrets to nation states like China. It would be foolish for someone to feel completely secure, given the news we read every day.

If my audience is more technically inclined or refuses to admit any weaknesses, I congratulate them on being ahead of the curve. I then continue my marketing efforts in other areas of the organization or begin reaching out to other prospects. There is no value in debating individuals who won't admit their weaknesses or remain loyal to another security provider.

When to Involve the Security Team

Finally, one last question always comes up: "When do I get the security teams involved, and do we continue to align our security team with the client's security team?" It's another great question.

Remember, bringing their security people in too early is an immediate demotion from the asset owner to the IT/ security organization—an introduction you don't yet want. In the coming chapters, we will address a sequence of events to help guide you through the selling process. This information provides you with the key principles for communicating with executives and asset owners: the people with liability.

Remember: Security is sold to asset owners, approved by IT decision makers, and implemented by security consultants from your organization. It can then be managed and maintained by your team or an internal security team. Selling to the security team is likely the biggest time waster when trying to close business.

CHAPTER FOURTEEN

An Incredible Security Value Proposition

> You have only a few seconds to turn short introductions or first-time meetings into strategic relationships. Security provides the perfect platform for doing just that.

Having an effective message may be the most important concept in this book. A speaker and friend of mine frequently asks, "What common task must you do uncommonly well if you are to succeed in business?"

He then offers the example of a surgeon. Picture a surgeon—someone who has trained for years to perform complex heart operations. You need surgery, and you've heard this guy is the best. His resume is outstanding, he's performed this procedure hundreds of times, and every operation has been a success.

You arrive early in the morning, ready for the procedure. The surgeon goes to work. He spends hours meticulously working to get every aspect of the operation just right, and finally he has solved the problem. He sews up the incision and, as he's leaving the OR, it suddenly occurs to him that he forgot to wash his hands.

Our family has spent many years building successful businesses. My father was an early entrepreneur. Throughout my childhood, I had the opportunity to watch him build his business. My brother-in-law has been doing the same for more than 20 years. And I too have followed this path. I've worked in several technology startups, as well as my current consulting and coaching practice. Continuing the legacy, I have involved my children in building businesses as part of their education. My sons and daughters have sewn clothes, run a horse back riding school, run a bakery, repaired and sold used bicycles, and trained dogs to name a few.

One of my sons has a business building a specialized calf-stretching wedge he distributes through physical therapy offices. One day early in my son's start-up phase, he came to me looking for ideas on how to expand his exercise-platform business. We talked about advertising, phonebook ads, signage and even cold calling.

I reminded him that his product sells primarily when a physical therapist recommends it to a patient. Not many people would really understand its value if he were to put up signs. But for some reason, when a doctor or physical therapist recommends something, we will pay hundreds of dollars for something as simple as a piece of plastic that sits in our shoe or for a pulley that hangs on a door to stretch a repaired rotator cuff. Somewhat disappointed, my son went on his way.

The next day, he came back to me, excited about a recent sale to a woman who exercises in our neighborhood. When I asked how he made the sale, he told me she walks down our road each day, so he decided to stop and talk to her about stretching. After a few minutes, she agreed to buy a wedge.

What was my son's value proposition? It's simple: He was 11. It's hard for people to turn down a young boy as he's building his own business.

Unfortunately, you and I aren't that cute. We have to come up with something that grabs the attention of adults who are too busy to stop and build a relationship with everyone they meet.

The Deadly Error of Having No Value Proposition

Let's take a real-world technology example. Over a decade ago, I served as vice president of a mid-size solution provider. I was responsible for bottom-line profitability. One day, while sitting in my office, my administrative assistance paged me, asking if I would join Bob, our sales manager, in the conference room. He needed my help ASAP.

When I arrived, I immediately saw the problem. Bob was sitting across the table from an engineer from a company that manufactures routers and switches. We already had a partnership with one of the largest providers of network technology, and this engineer was working hard to convince Bob that his technology was superior. With very limited network experience, Bob sat with a glazed look on his face. As I sat down, I noticed two other men in the room dressed in suits.

I let them go on for about five minutes before interrupting the engineer to reintroduce everyone. I quickly learned that we had a local channel manager, regional manager and the speaker, an engineer from South Carolina.

Once introduced, the engineer started again, but I quickly interrupted him. Looking over at the regional manager, I had one simple question: "How are we going to make more money in the coming year if we take on this product"? The regional manager looked over at the engineer and began to explain that his company's superior technology was a sure winner and asked that we continue the technical overview.

Looking again at the manager I said, "Well, that isn't really what I'm asking. I want to know how I'm going to make more incremental income if we take on this product." He was taken aback by the question, not understanding why the technology didn't interest me. I explained that we were selling a lot of our current partner's product, and I didn't really understand how this product would turn into more money.

He didn't have an answer for me. At that point, I thought it was best to end the meeting and have them go back to their office and find an answer. I promised I would make time to meet again when they had one. It's been over fifteen years since they left my office, and I still haven't heard back from them. I'm starting to think they may never call back. Actually, I think they failed to develop a value proposition that mattered to the economic buyer.

The Undeniable Importance of a Value Proposition

You meet new contacts every day. It may be in a large enterprise account, mid-sized account, or the SMB. You see them at trade shows, marketing events, association meetings, in hallways and in meetings you attend. But what happens to them? Chances are most of them never turn into anything more than a one-time contact.

If you learn one thing from this book, it should be the importance of building effective messaging. When I work with resellers on building their security and managed services business, I ask them to write down what they tell people when they're introduced or when answering the question, "What do you do"? If you work for a manufacturer, at least you have a brand. But as a solution provider, you really have nothing outside the intellectual capital you and your teams possess to solve business problems. Creating differentiation is the key. In the next chapter we will take a look at what potential clients really care about.

CHAPTER FIFTEEN

IT Doesn't Care

> IT people don't have liability. They don't really care about security. They care about job stability, quality of life, income and benefits, and the appreciation they get from management.

IT Personnel Don't Care About Business

When I refer to IT personnel, I'm not talking about CIOs. I mean the average IT office workers—people who oversee networks and systems. In my workshops we usually have a lively discussion about what the IT person really cares about.

If you've never worked on the IT side of the business, you may be in for a shock. It's not about schedules, best price, or gaining efficiencies. Sure, there are exceptions to the rule, but of the many people who have come up the ranks from IT, it seems the average IT worker is mostly concerned with the following: compensation, building a great resume, having less work to do, getting into the right cubicle, free lunches, golf outings, and perhaps most important, access to cool technology.

With technology, we're not talking about the mission-critical systems, but the new high-tech offerings and access to smart technical people that allow IT people to learn and enhance their resumes. And if they could somehow reach a level in their career where they have their own CAN—(cubicle area network); you know, with the coolest laptop, the most memory, etc., this is real status. Having their own printer, file server, router, etc., right in their own cubicle is the dream of every IT custodian.

So why do we spend so much time negotiating with, and writing detailed proposals for these people? The negotiation dance you're going through with IT is really their way of feeling powerful. In the end, the percent-off doesn't matter; this person has no budget and has nothing to gain if they save or spend a few dollars.

Learn how you can help IT people become successful, and you will win the trust and friendship you're looking for—if you can deliver it. But don't mistake them for the buyer.

Department Managers Care About Their Business

Unlike IT people, managers on the profit-center side of the business have budgets and financial goals that earn them bonuses and reputation. This is where you often find buyers who are also early adopters of technology. These people are asset owners. If they can find new technology that puts them ahead of the competition, they are likely to buy it. Most sales people have completely missed this side of the sales equation. It's time to get out there and meet the people that make money for the company. These are your best and most powerful influencers.

CXO Executives Are Changing Roles

There may be various terms or descriptions used for C-Levels, but the bottom line is shareholder value. This is true primarily for

CEOs and SMB Business Owners.

CIOs are also asset owners as we've already noted. The CIO role is changing as I am writing this. According to the WSJ, every major decision must go through the CIO office because every major decision relies on technology. There's no clear line between business decisions and IT decisions any more. Another thing to keep in mind, according to Forrester Research, is that the CIO office still controls the majority of the IT budget.

The CIO profile is also changing. Companies are upgrading their CIOs. The old profile of a data center or data processing manager is over. The board is looking for people who can take the company forward. People with business acumen who will move from pure operational tasks to strategic initiatives that involve and enable sales and marketing, and customer experience. Companies are looking for competitive advantage and operational efficiency, and they are hoping technology can deliver it.

Amazon.com is a great example. Years ago, they started out as a book store. Today they look more like a technology company than anything. They compete with Wal*Mart, but they are so much more. They sell just about everything. But they also provide cloud apps, cloud storage, online music, video libraries, and more. People join Amazon, paying $99 to become a Prime Member. The question every company should be asking is, "How do we become the next Amazon.com? How do we get our customers to pay to shop and shop here first?"

The question you should be asking is, "How can you become the trusted advisor of the next Amazon.com?"

CISOs Are Also Changing and Are Rapidly Being Replaced

The CISO role is also changing. What used to be a technical position is now being called a risk position. Compliance is important, but maintaining security is more important. The Board needs someone who can give them the information they need to make fast, safe decisions.

When talking with directors, you should be able to rattle their primary needs as I've discussed them, showing them the impact vs. likelihood chart, and explaining where security is headed. As I have done this in recent meetings, I've been able to establish immediate credibility. Many IT and Security directors don't really understand what I'm saying, but it suddenly makes sense when talking to an asset owner. Suddenly they wish they had this kind of information.

CHAPTER SIXTEEN

What's A Trusted Advisor?

> It's an overused term that's becoming meaningless. Can we inject some new life into this term? In fact we can. It may be overused but it's underserved. Take a look at what it should mean.

The Right Definition of "Trusted Advisor"

"Trusted advisor" may be an overused term—one that has lost its original meaning. Sales reps use it to refer to just about every relationship they have. Somehow sales reps have embraced the idea they can go out and be a customer's trusted advisor without really trying. They can't. Asset Owners choose their advisors.

The asset owner relies on this individual. As the name implies, the trusted advisor must be trustworthy and capable of advising. This seems simple—perhaps even silly when you first read it. The "trusted" part of the phrase should be a given, but many salespeople are not trustworthy.

What about the concept of "advisor"? Do you have knowledge a client would value, for which he'd be willing to pay? Think for a moment of all the salespeople who have called on you in the last few years. Were they able to "advise" you? If you're going to move into this highly regarded position, you must have some intellectual capital that matters to clients. If you simply sell storage, networks, servers or other hardware and software products, chances are you have nothing on which to advise your clients. Perhaps your only value at this point is to supply products at reasonable prices—not a long-term position of strength.

Earlier I spoke about learning the sound bites to sound like the expert. That's a great start. "I believe that 30% of the technology sales force will go away over the next 5 years," Mack Hanan, author of *Consultative Selling*, told me years ago over a dinner meeting in New York. His comments come from watching the commoditization of technology hardware. Most executives today can operate without advice when it comes to building networks, installing servers, and bringing in basic infrastructure.

It's been more than five years, and perhaps Mack overstated his position, but as companies continue to make it easier to implement these technologies, I believe that more sales will be conducted over the Internet, with the IT department doing more of the installation or just using the cloud. To stay on top, you the seller must get serious about being that expert that sits between product features and business enablement. You must become the buyer's risk advisor.

When I conduct security workshops, salespeople frequently comment, "I don't want to become a security expert; I have consultants who does that." The problem with this attitude is that salespeople are still under the impression they can build relationships with executives just by being friendly and helpful. Every company has friendly sales people. There's no differentiation here – being friendly and helpful is not a value proposition unless if comes with some substance. Check out what Matthew Dixon and Brent Adamson say about this in their book,

The Challenger Sale.

Who Pick's The Trusted Advisor?

A friend from the National Speakers Association (NSA) once shared a story about his rise from failure to success. Art was part of a safety organization, working for the railroad. He eventually left to become a motivational speaker. At first, it was hard to find work, but one of his colleagues encouraged him to become more of an advisor by specializing. He said, "The world doesn't need another generic motivational speaker."

Looking for ways to accomplish this, Art began to study transportation safety "sound bites." He took the most pressing issues and frequently asked questions and began studying and memorizing sound-bite answers. When he spoke, he spoke with authority, quoting the sources people recognized. Before long he sounded like an expert.

Overnight, Art's name was getting out. Suddenly he was being interviewed on radio programs, speaking at events and being asked for advice. Over the next few years he became one of the most highly paid safety-expert speakers in the NSA.

Art's story isn't unique. I've heard similar tales from others, and I've done it myself. By using sound bites from the WSJ and other sources respected by business leaders you can begin speaking with authority. But it's more than sound bites. Once you get started and really focus on an area, you start picking up new truths wherever you go. You meet others in the same field with more expertise or different experiences, and you begin learning from each other. The more you meet with others, the more you learn. Over time, you really do become the expert. But the key is focus and studying the resources around you.

At this point I feel it's important to point out how many sales people are unwilling to spend any of their own money on self improvement. If they have to spend $500 to subscribe to the WSJ, it's out of the question. And when it comes to hiring a coach or joining a study group or group coaching program, they won't do it if the company won't let them expense it. Consider this. If you spent $10,000 on an annual coaching program, one great idea in that one year would easily pay your annual fee. It's simple return on investment. Investing in yourself is the most important investment you can make if you want to move up to that advisor status.

When it comes time to meet with your new prospects, you get a about 30 minutes with the asset owner. Your job is to sell him on the concepts presented here and introduce your technical people to him when it's time. You come with a strategic level of knowledge that gets things started, turning over the more technical details to your engineering staff.

The key point here: Clients will choose advisors based on what they need to know to be successful. The advisor will be invited to planning meetings, have insights into where the organization is going, and will be the one consulted when decisions are made.

The relevance to security is this: Asset owners need help in making sure their assets are safe. They won't go to their own IT people. They need someone from the outside who they can trust. That person needs to be you, which moves you from a vendor to an advisor.

The things that will help you become a trusted advisor may include your industry knowledge in a vertical market like healthcare, references that show you've been successful with other clients, product knowledge, awareness of what's happening in the security market, and knowledge of the cyber-crime world.

Clients will ultimately choose their trusted advisors. Will you be one of them?

CHAPTER SEVENTEEN

Can You Answer the Question?

> What do you do? It's one of the most frequently asked questions in business today. Can you answer the question? When you answer does it lead to relationship or silence?

Two Components of Your Value Proposition

Your Value Proposition is what takes price off the table. Just about everything you sell is a commodity. You might think your people or your certifications make you unique, they don't. You meet prospects every day. What happens to them? In the last 12 months, I've added about 500 names to my database, but can I phone these people next week and get them to take my call? Will they remember who I am? Are they willing to meet with me if I do call?

In my coaching practice, I frequently ask salespeople if their list of prospects is made of real relationships, or are they mere acquaintances? In most cases, the latter is true. How can you begin to change this trend and start turning introductions into meaningful relationships?

The Problem with your Elevator Pitch

Most of us have been given an elevator pitch—something developed by our marketing group to explain what we do in a few seconds. The pitch has to be quick enough to share in an elevator—high impact, but to the point. The problem with most elevator pitches is they're all about us. A salesperson will say, "Let me tell you how great I am so you can buy something from me."

One day, I was in an elevator with the president and CEO of a nation-wide bank I worked for. I'd just had my review, and while my marks were excellent, I was somewhat disappointed with my title and income level. There we were, just the two of us, and I thought to myself, "What can I say to get this person to see my value?" I couldn't come up with anything meaningful. Now, looking back, I realize why. Anything I said would have sounded like a sales pitch. The CEO would have likely seen it as a cheap attempt to point out my greatness, and he would have quickly dismissed it as a character flaw.

An elevator pitch is like throwing up on someone. It doesn't feel good, and it doesn't have a positive outcome. It is usually filled with esoteric language, industry vernacular and meaningless jargon.

The Most Effective Value Proposition

The value proposition is different. It's an introduction that gives someone an understanding of what you can do for him. It's focused on his needs—a brief description of the benefits you can bring. It's not a list of features, so if you're going to provide this benefit statement, it's essential to have some idea of what the potential client needs before you start talking.

The value proposition is a powerful way to share your worth with a client, but he has to be ready to hear it. He has to ask for it. This is the key: getting the prospect or client to ask you for your value. This is what gives you permission to answer with power.

Two Essential Parts of the Value Proposition

I like to break messaging into two parts. First comes the advisory positioning statement (what I call the APS), a quick way to position myself with a potential client. It must be short enough to be an introduction, yet provide sufficient content to grab the person's interest. It must move him to ask the question, "What is your value proposition?" By doing this, I gain the listener's attention, which in turn creates an opportunity for me to deliver an effective value proposition.

The Advisory Positioning Statement

The advisory positioning statement is my introduction. I use it in hallways, at meetings where I have just a moment to speak, or when meeting someone at an association event or conference. It's the short one-minute introduction that allows me to grab his attention.

What's the question most often asked? "What do you do?" Can you answer it? If you look at most introductions, they don't actually amount to anything. They're weak! "I'm in sales." Okay, now what?

You are introduced to someone's coworker, colleague or manager, and you introduce yourself as a salesperson or consultant – what do you expect to happen after that? If you are thinking, you'll ask for a card. But from there, it's all chance. You might follow up with an email, or you might even place a call if you are really proactive. But in most cases, nothing happens. So, how do you turn this around and make it something more strategic?

Give Me Green Grass Not Grass Seed and Manure

If you've ever been to North Carolina, you know there is a lot of red clay. It's nearly impossible to grow grass without spending a lot of time and money. If you were to look over my yard, it's like looking over a desert. The clay soil is hard and barren. Big weeds sprout from crevasses that form from the intense heat. Then there are the huge mounds of fire-ant hills that never go away, no matter how much poison you use. Each year, I plant grass, it rains, the seeds wash into the woods, and I am left with what looks like a scene from an Arizona's desert.

A while back, I received a note in the mail that advertised a lawn-care service that would come to my property and analyze my grass. It was a free assessment. I thought this would be a great way to get some answers. When the person arrived he began to analyze my yard. Once the assessment was complete, he came to the door to deliver the bad news.

Before letting Scott, our local grass specialist begin, I asked him about his value proposition. I clearly caught him off guard with this question, but he finally responded with his tagline, "Chemlawn is where lawns mean more."

"Scott, that's not a value proposition, it's a tagline" I replied. "What value can you give me?"

Looking at my yard, I placed my hand on Scott's shoulder and said, "Scott, look at my lawn. You know how hard it is to grow grass in North Carolina"?

"Yes, we have a program to fix this," he said.

"Scott, that is your value proposition," I informed him. "If you had come to me and said, 'Dave, you know how hard it is to grow grass out here in this heat?' I would have said, 'Yes, look at my yard.' "

Scott could have empathized with me, saying "I see the problem. Our team has developed a unique solution. I specialize in fixing this problem!" And I would have replied, "Show me what it is!"

You know how hard it is for companies to know who is accessing specific data at any given time?

You know how difficult it is for companies to put in proactive, detection oriented security solutions, that provide the intelligence needed to protect the assets?

You know how hard it is to make sure every system that connects to a company's network—whether a laptop, remote user, partner, third-party consultant, or customer is who they say they are, and isn't doing anything he's unauthorized to do?

You know how hard it is to detect someone doing something he shouldn't be doing, and to stop him before he damages or steals something?

If you could come up with a simple question that starts with "You know how…,"—one that resonates with the person you are meeting and causes him to say, "Yeah, that's the problem. We struggle with that all the time."—you would have an opportunity to say, "This is what I focus on. There is a solution."

This prompts the client to ask for the program or process developed to fix the problem—a unique, yet affordable, process. It gets him to ask you for your value proposition. And once I asked about the program, Scott was in a position to share his value proposition with my undivided attention.

Using My APS in Real Life

Several years ago I had the opportunity to meet a channel executive from a large software company. My contact, a channel manager in the mid-Atlantic, asked me if I'd like to meet his manager. I was excited about the opportunity, until he then told me the meeting would take place at a trade show—a forum of thousands of custodians milling around, hunting for free T-shirts and pens. I would have to buy my own airline ticket and spend the day traveling for a short meeting amid chaos. Was this a good opportunity?

I took the chance, thinking this is my only opportunity. When I arrived, it was lunchtime and, as I had predicted, we were surrounded by noise and confusion. My contact brought me to the restaurant where his manager was eating with a group of people, another obstacle to any meeting with a purpose. But look at what happened next.

I extended my welcome to the East Coast Channel Manager, leading with my name, followed by my APS. (You know how difficult it is to get your resellers to understand the value message of your organization? They seem to focus on the commodity products, leaving out the most important aspects of your program.)

Jim' s eyes lit up. He said, "Yes, that is the problem."

"That is what I focus on," I quickly replied.

"Really!" he said. "Tell me what you do."

I told him I'd show him, but we would need to set up a short meeting at his office to go over it. We arranged the meeting, but it didn't end there.

In the follow-up meeting, he called his manager (the North America's Channel Manager) and asked him to meet with me. We set the meeting for a few weeks later.

As I sat down in his office, his first question was: "Dave, what is your value proposition?"

I almost fell out of my chair when I heard those words. He later introduced me to his global manager, and we started discussing a very large nationwide opportunity—one worth a lot of money. And it all came from a simple APS delivered in the midst of a chaotic trade show.

In another situation, I had a slightly different experience. The vice president at a major security manufacturing company had asked me to speak at his national partner conference. The dates didn't work for me, so I had to decline. But as I was planning my next year's speaking calendar, I called him. His administrative assistant informed me my contact was no longer there, but a replacement had started two weeks ago. She patched me through, and I found myself talking to the new VP of marketing.

At some point in the conversation, I mentioned the word "training" (immediate delegation to the training department). I felt myself sinking. But then I remembered the the APS, "You know how…" I mentioned some of the issues her channel was facing. Her excitement seemed to kick in as she said, "Yes, that is the issue."

" That is what I focus on," I replied.

She immediately changed her tone and invited me to take a look at some slides she was preparing for the upcoming XChange conference in Chicago. She was asking me to become an advisor.

There were several points I didn't agree with, having worked with many resellers around the country. When we were done, she said, "I want to meet with you when I return." She was inviting me to continue in that advisory role, and I was asked to share my value proposition.

This brings us to the next step: We must have an answer. If people are going to ask us for the value prop, our response has to knock them off their chair.

The Art of Creating an Effective Value Proposition

Once your APS is perfected, people will ask you for your value proposition. In fact, it is important that you constantly test the APS questions to see how people respond. Just like in our discussion on direct response marketing, conversion is what matters here. If you're not converting people from saying hello to asking for your value proposition, you're wasting your time.

Are they asking for more, or are they exchanging a pleasant smile and walking away? If they aren't asking, your questions need work. But once they start asking, you will need a response. When the software channel executive asked, I only had one chance—and it had to be perfect.

The security value proposition is likely the most powerful value proposition available in today's market. But before we can actually build one, we need to review some of the theory behind it. First, let's look at how security is positioned in the market and how it can be changed to create more impact at the business level.

CHAPTER EIGHTEEN

Security Is Not Insurance:

> Nobody wants to buy more insurance. If you're treating security like an insurance sale, you'll probably starve to death. There has to be a better way. Let's take a look.

It's been said, "Security has no ROI." Others have come along and tried to show it does, or that there is a *return on not investing*. Both may hold some truth, but neither is helpful. Let's look at it from another angle.

Consider a sport like rock-climbing. If you climb, you know it involves equipment, your body, and the rock. The climber wants to do something that, in many ways, seems to be impossible. He takes on cliffs that are thousands of feet tall and overhangs that defy gravity. He may spend his nights sleeping while suspended from ropes anchored by small metal objects placed in rock cracks.

To achieve this, the climber invests in ropes, camming devices (chocks in the old days), carabiners that clip things together, special shoes, a helmet, and a sling to carry his gear. When the ascent begins, the climber wears the harness and begins to place metal anchors into the rock as he works his way up. With the exception of the shoes, the gear is never actually used to support the climber, unless he falls. All gear is designed for safety—not insurance. If the climber falls, the rope, belayed by a teammate, will tighten, held by the anchors in the rock, and will support the climber, stopping the fall. He invests in safety so he can mitigate risk and decrease danger. And this allows him to do what seems impossible.

Business Safety vs. Cyber-Insurance

This analogy carries over to corporations looking to extend their safe business practices into less secure environments that will produce greater profitability. Some are sending their sales force on the road to access secure corporate systems from insecure wireless locations. They work out of airports, coffee shops, hotels and even citywide wireless access points. Businesses may allow guest users, third-party processing companies, supply chain management applications, and customer online access. All of these activities expose the company to the risk of unauthorized users gaining access through compromised systems. Newer technology initiatives involving app stores, cloud, BYOD, and collaboration make these measures even more critical.

Rock climbers enjoy purchasing safety equipment. They look for new technologies that will provide greater security, allowing them to take on bigger challenges. The change from chocks to cams in the mid-'80s, for example, was an expensive upgrade for most of us, but we went for it, knowing these new devices would be less likely to fail. We could then take greater chances out on the rock face.

If we can convince our customers to view security in this way, there's an opportunity to apply the security/safety net to new business applications, enabling them to reach farther than they ever imagined.

Take a moment and consider several accounts you are working with right now. Every business that uses technology in any significant way is doing things to extend its business—to reach out to new markets, collaborate with partners who many times also compete, or perhaps outsourcing or offshoring to gain efficiencies in manufacturing or call center activities. All of these things introduce new levels of risk. What are your clients doing with their business to become more competitive or more efficient. How are these things introducing new risks? Write down several ideas. We will use them to create an effective, business-focused value proposition.

Find the "Unique Thing" in Your Business

The next step, before we can actually build the value proposition or an opening to a more formal dialogue about your value, must be to understand what's really unique about your company. Have you ever tried to make a list of things that are truly unique about your organization? It's not an easy task. When I work with manufacturers, I hear comments like, "We have an end-to-end solution" or "Our support is better than any other company's." Perhaps they say, "Our thought leadership is better" or "We are setting the standards in the industry." When I hear this, my immediate thought is: "How will the executive of a large corporation receive these ideas?"

Do you have security solutions that span the network, mainframe, operating systems, applications, databases, and end users? When you really think about it, there aren't too many true end-to-end solutions out there. Or, how about "best customer support, leadership and expertise?" Can you really make this claim—and can you prove it? Most prospects won't just believe you.

How about resellers? Do you have the best people, support, or another unique qualification? In most cases, these things don't work. Everyone says they have great people and multiple certifications. Most resellers look exactly alike on paper.

As a manufacturer, you have to consider the security aspects you can provide that no other company offers—perhaps a set of products that work together in a unique way. If you work for an operating-system company like Microsoft or provide one of the various UNIX platforms, you can claim you're the only one who can really secure that system. Or, if you are a storage or network manufacturer, you may be able to claim that only you can provide security inside the devices you sell, thus leveraging your client's current investment in infrastructure.

As a reseller, you may have a particular methodology that has been developed to assess security. You may have a specialized security managed-services program developed for a certain market—perhaps even a vertical market. These are all unique.

In either type of company you have references. Everyone has references, but your references are unique. Your team's experience is unique to your company. And while other companies may make similar claims, the culture you build—whether an advantage or a liability—is, in fact, unique. Get a list. Brainstorm and come up with ideas that make you unique, and start building more differentiation into your company.

But at the top of the list is *you*—you as a trusted advisor. If you take the time to become the advisor—if you start identifying and memorizing the sound bites—you will be unique. The is what *The Challenger Sale* is all about. Most salespeople won't do this, so take a step past your competitors and equip yourself with the one thing executives will notice.

Only a Few Things Really Interest Executives

Now, with some level of differentiation, you need to ask the question: "What's really interesting to executives?" Again, a list is important. You have only one chance to connect with these people. It has to be perfect. Over the last two years, I have compiled a list from technology sellers I've worked with. Here's a partial list of what we came up with:

- ☐ Security trends—what's really happening globally.
- ☐ What peers and competitors are doing to reduce risk.
- ☐ How companies are reducing the cost of security.
- ☐ Where and why security strategies are failing.
- ☐ How to reduce the risk of exposure.
- ☐ How to reduce the liability associated with loss.
- ☐ The futures—where security and cyber-crime are headed.
- ☐ What is hype, and what is reality?
- ☐ How does cloud change security?
- ☐ Is BYOD really safe?

Recall what the Wall Street Journal says executives are interested in (or want to know):

- ☐ What are the top 5 to 7 threats our company faces?
- ☐ What are the odds we'll be compromised by these threats over the next 12 months?
- ☐ Are we trending up or down?
- ☐ How are we managing to this?

These areas continue to be interesting to executives. As I get involved in marketing events (Lunch & Learns,) seminars, and other speaking opportunities, I consistently find executives are willing to attend events where we address these issues. On the other hand, when I speak at or attend events that are more application-oriented or product-focused, the audience is almost completely made up of technical non-decision makers.

With this in mind, look back at your recent meetings. Are these the topics you're leading with, or are you resorting to Power Point slides, product data sheets, and other technical information? In my experience, most salespeople focus on the wrong issues, leading with their comfort zone and pushing the products with which they have been working. These conversations quickly move to the technical audience, leaving the decision makers out of the discussion. It's an immediate delegation back to the IT group.

In the next chapter, we will take a look at when and how to get their technical people involved, but at this stage our focus is on creating a vision for security at a business level—a vision in the mind of the asset owner.

CHAPTER NINETEEN

How to Build Your Value Proposition:

> Everyone has an elevator pitch of some kind. In most cases you've been given one from your marketing people. The elevator pitch is like throwing up on your client – and then asking them to buy.

The Components of Your Value Proposition

We can now begin to build our value proposition. The APS may have been used in a brief introduction, or someone may have sponsored you to meet with senior managers, economic buyers or high-level influencers. However you got the meeting, you now have one chance to make it count. So, what do you do?

Let's face it, every sales methodology out there calls for meeting the decision maker or economic buyer. While I agree with this process, it means you and every other salesperson in the marketplace are calling one of two key individuals on every deal. The result? Thousands of salespeople are calling on a few key executives, who are tired of meeting salespeople with nothing important to say. The bottom line: You really need something great.

I've developed a short, five-point outline for the value proposition that takes the focus off the product (and the product people in the room), while placing the emphasis on key business systems and data. This immediately calls for the executive's attention. Let's look at the outline:

- ☐ Security Trends
- ☐ What I See (Impact)
- ☐ My Concern
- ☐ What We Are Doing
- ☐ Specific to You

Security Trends. Security trends are a great place to start. We covered much of this in earlier chapters, but current news is important. This is not a scare tactic, but an articulation of the power, resources and determination behind organized crime, and today's primary threat actors.

People love news. We have 24/7 news channels, all kinds of newspapers and magazines, and hours of talk radio, all delivering updates and commentary. Current security news gives your audience something relevant and interesting to focus on, while linking it to the data and risk of loss your prospect may be up against.

What I See (Impact). Working each day with systems and networks, you should be seeing the impact of these trends. Your consultants are likely watching as companies are hit with data loss, system outages, liability exposure, failed audits, and possible business failure when they don't take the necessary steps to secure their systems and data. Review this with your prospect in a few short sentences to show you're witnessing the "bad guys" winning this battle. This should be a fairly short statement of the bad things you see as companies do the wrong thing.

My Concern. Your Transition. Security is your global humanitarian concern. At this point you might want to shed a tear (not literally, but verbally). You should be passionate about people taking action, showing the same zeal as those who want to save trees, animals, starving children, and cancer patients.

You need to convey the following message: If someone doesn't come up with a way to stop security breaches, real companies could be out of business, banks could fail, and utilities could face major outages. Your personal identity could be stolen, and people could destroy your credit ratings, costing you and your family unfathomable recovery time and money. Remember, millions of identities around the world have been exposed in the last year. This is a serious issue. You communicate this with a short statement, "I am really concerned about this – companies are losing the battle."

What We Are Doing About It. Someone has to solve your clients' problems. The steps companies are currently taking are failing. Data is being compromised, identities are being stolen, and information is being misused. Your company must build or supply some unique solution.

Remember the house model: protection, detection, and response. These are the key aspects of security. How is your company working toward fixing the problem? Are you building security right into your product? Are you providing a way for smaller organizations to affordably apply the right kind of security? Or are you helping companies bring intelligent response to their data defense system? This is where you articulate that value differentiation list we made a few pages back.

Specific to You. The last part of this meeting involves applying your solution to something that motivates the client to spend the next 30 minutes talking about his problems and your solutions. Look back at the safety issues you came up with for your client. Are they worth spending 30 minutes on? If they are business-oriented, relevant issues, your prospect should have no problem spending at least 30 minutes looking at how your offerings fit with his business direction.

Build it - Memorize It!

Now that you have an outline, here comes the hard part: writing a compelling value proposition. An example for a typical network company or solution provider might sound something like this:

"Before we talk about our company and what we offer, I'd like to take a minute to share with you what we're seeing. Security challenges are changing. Intellectual property theft is growing at an alarming rate, as organized crime recognizes it as a Trillion-dollar market. As with identity theft years ago, nation-states are building huge programmer work forces to take control of companies like yours. They want ideas and innovations.

According to the U.S. Department of Defense, every major company in the country has been compromised at this point.

I am concerned as I observe our national accounts experiencing these types of problems. Last year, well secured organizations including the Pentagon, the CIA, the FBI, and NASA were all successfully infiltrated despite multimillion dollar security budgets. But what about all of the companies that don't even know they have been compromised? It is estimated that malware sits dormant in a company like yours for 250 days on average before doing anything - and you won't don't find out for an average of 14 *months. It took TJ Max three years and 100 million credit cards before knowing, and Target 40 million card numbers and 110 identities – costing them over $1.4 million to recover.*

At our company we are very concerned about this. We have dedicated vast resources and money to fix this issue. We believe that if we can build the security to stop such threats into the infrastructure or network you have already purchased, many of these problems can be fixed. If we create a way to detect and respond to infected computers, unauthorized users, and intruders with malicious intent before they reach your data, we can stop much of what we're seeing.

As I've worked with your company, I see you use a lot of third-party processing. You use business process outsourcing and BYOD applications. Some of the advances we are making in this area of security can greatly enhance the level of security in your organization. In the same way you are protecting systems and servers with antivirus and spyware protection, we can protect the actual network within your organization. I would like to spend the next 30 minutes to examine how this may apply to your business more specifically, and if it makes sense, create some next steps. How does this sound to you?"

It Must Be Predictable

Be willing to spend sufficient time on your proposition. It must read well to get the response you're looking for, and you have to deliver it as though it's a part of you. As with any successful movie, the script has to be developed, and the actor needs to study and memorize it. Finally, it has to be rehearsed. Then, as you deliver it, it will adapt. You will ultimately be capable of changing it as new situations arise. Above all, don't be lazy here. Many people assume they can pull it off without preparing. They think they can wing it. But can you imagine watching a movie with no script, where the actors make up dialogue as they go along? I'm guessing it wouldn't be a hit.

Your proposition must sound as though it came from you—not from your marketing group.

Set Up the Meeting to Ask Questions

Your value proposition sets the agenda, naturally leading to the first question: **"What are you trying to protect?"** It moves you from product to asset, starting with the news and ending with a business application. The first question then reinforces this move, shifting conversation away from the technical people in the room and toward the businesspeople who can make buying decisions.

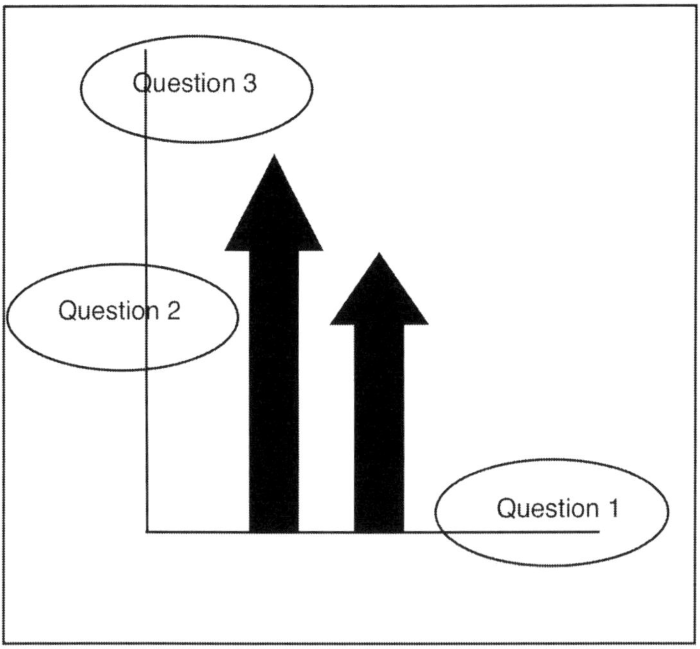

Figure: Impact vs. Likelihood

You can then ask the second question: **"What are the relevant threats?"** This prompts data owners to share the areas in which they feel vulnerable.

Finally, you can ask: **"How comfortable are you with your organization's ability to detect and respond to attacks?"**

These questions uncover the critical assets, relevant threats, and the company's posture, which helps you build the Impact vs. Likelihood Graph.

This is a dialogue— a rapport-building process that allows you to exchange ideas and see the situation from the client's perspective. Once you have this, it's time to start bringing things to a close with some action items. "Discussion" comes from a word that means "to end the dialogue"— it's time now for a discussion and the house model.

The House, The Cloud and The Coverage Model can now be used to show clients where their security strategies are weak, how easy it is to break in, and what holistic security should look like. From here, we will look at what to do with this information and how to create justification to move security initiatives forward.

CHAPTER TWENTY

Creating Undeniable Justification:

> Security never depends on budget – Move your client away from thinking "product" and toward the risk associated with assets. Then work to provide a clear measure of risk – a measure of impact vs. likelihood.

Undeniable justification is built when the client sees imminent danger. The security sale is powerful simply because every company you deal with has inadequate security protection. And they always will because the hackers are always one step ahead. As technologies continue to evolve, providing more DETECTION type controls, you'll be constantly upgrading your client to more sophisticated, and perhaps remotely managed security systems.

I'll never forget the sales call I had with an electronics manufacturer in the southeast. After weeks of trying to get a meeting, we finally made our way in to see the CIO and several members of the IT support staff. It seemed like every question we came up with, and every issue we referenced, they "Had it covered."

After about 45 minutes of this back and forth conversation, we were clearly headed nowhere. This meeting was a waste of time. Gathering our documents, I made one last ditch effort. Looking at the CIO I simply said, "It sounds like your team has it covered. It's amazing to me when a small company like yours has such a sophisticated security strategy. Over the past year NASA, the Pentagon, the FBI, and the CIA have all been compromised. I don't think I've even been inside a company that had better security than these organizations."

On my way out he stopped me. "We need to talk," he said. Apparently his team thought they had it covered, but he wasn't so sure. Finally we were ready to engage is some truthful conversation.

Compliance and Cyber Crime Threats Don't Create Business – So What Does?

IT People, according to the recent reports from the Wall Street Journal, are afraid to admit they have security problems. So, where do you take these meetings? If compliance and cyber-crime are not sufficient motivators, what will create justification for a security sale?

Two Powerful Pathways to New Opportunities :

1. **Demand Generation Events:** In my Event Marketing Success Kit, I lay out a complete strategy for inviting key decision makers to an educational event, with a well planned program that will convert them to clients using risk assessments. On average we see conversion rates of 75% or more from attending to participating in the assessment process.

2. **Client Business Initiatives:** Companies all around us are in the process of migrating to new, disruptive technology applications. We see a tremendous migration to cloud, BYOD (Bring Your Own Device,) big data, and collaborative technologies. Each of these represents a major change in computing architecture, requiring a new look at security.

In either case, asset risk levels are affected, and there's an opportunity to review key concepts with clients. Notice that we're not waiting for them to initiate the requisition of security product. That's the third way to sell, but not a good one. Product proposals without proper justification only lead to price wars.

The Right Kind of Assessments Justify Spending

I recommend that your first sale with this client be an assessment. For decades, salespeople have used assessments to justify spending, so this is not a new concept. A well qualified, asset-owner-level assessment, will lead to new business 90% of the time.

By doing this, you avoid the long sales cycles associated with large product sales or even new technology or project sales. The sales time is spent selling a small assessment that's easy to approve without going to the board. Once in motion, justification can be established for an unlimited number of projects and services to follow. We will cover this in more detail shortly.

Using a complementary assessment, your sales team can maintain complete control over the process. Since the client hasn't paid for the assessment, you control who must be involved. If the right people don't participate, simply stop the process.

Let's take a look at how assessments are conducted and what constitutes a strong business case for moving security projects forward. While it is not within the scope of this book to explain the full assessment process and deliverables, it's important to differentiate it from routine vulnerability assessments frequently delivered to the IT organization.

When I was working with the small bank referenced earlier in the book, the executive VP asked me for my recommendation on what to do next. He needed to know what to do next to move from a protection-only strategy to the PDR model I described: I recommended an assessment; however, it occurred to me he might have already conducted one.

"If you already have this type of data, I can use it," I told him. "But first let me review some of the different approaches security providers take when performing an assessment to see if your data will meet our needs."

Most companies today are conducting some type of regular security assessment, however, in most cases they are looking at the wrong things. The results are meaningless - leaving executives in the dark as to what their real situation looks like.

Vulnerability Assessment

Talking to the VP at the bank, I first addressed vulnerability. When consultants perform a security assessment, they usually focus most of their efforts on discovering vulnerabilities. This may include unpatched systems, misconfigured firewalls, sloppy application security, or a lack of hardening on the servers, among other issues.

While the vulnerability assessment has some value, the documents produced from these initiatives are generally too technical and largely useless to senior managers. The problem is, few consultants understand how to turn this data into actionable intelligence. As a result, vulnerabilities are prioritized (maybe) and delivered straight to IT. They may read them, but in most cases this report will be relegated to someone's shelf for a period of time, and eventually move on to become someone's landfill.

Consider your doctor. Imagine your next physical as a routine security or health assessment. But think of it in terms of a health vulnerability assessment. He'll run a bunch of tests and provide a list of every vitamin deficiency, germ exposure, cancer risk, or injury possibility. This list would obviously be quite long. And it would be almost useless. In most cases the blood work would look more like an excerpt from a Latin text book, than usable health information. Most of us look for the obvious familiar numbers such as cholesterol and triglycerides. The rest just sits on the shelf.

Penetration Test

Sometimes used interchangeably with vulnerability assessments, a penetration test, or Pen test, is a completely different animal. Here, you're focusing on specific systems or data, with the intent to break in. A client may hire you to try to steal data (sometimes called trophies) to see if you can break through their security barriers.

I had one client in Florida working with a healthcare organization. The IT guy wanted my client to quote on a pen test opportunity. In our next coaching session we were discussing this opportunity. My first question was, "Why does he specifically want a pen test?" My client wasn't sure, but without this information it would be impossible to create the justification needed to win the deal. In our next session he came back with, "To prove to their clients that the healthcare systems are secure." It was a move to demonstrate greater security as a competitive advantage. This kind of thinking is completely wrong. In the end we quoted a high number without doing any more fact finding or proposal writing. Here's why.

My client's IT contact claimed he had approval and signature authority. He wanted a pen test to prove he was secure. Our strategy was to find the real decision makers. We explained that this approach would only end in us breaking in. Our position was that a strong pen test team can always get in. The purpose of a pen test is to prove the vulnerability exists, not to see if a company can be breached.

Pen tests are expensive. They require extensive planning to ensure the business isn't disrupted. There is benefit to them, particularly when executives don't believe a system can be penetrated, but in most cases they are used to prove out certain vulnerabilities. Experienced security professionals never believe that a system is actually impenetrable.

But in the drive to sell products, solutions, and perhaps managed services, this test is not the best way to provide justification. In fact, all it does is prove what we already know: that someone out there can break in. And if we can't get through, it merely means we didn't have the right people on our team. The client has gained nothing from this.

As I explained this to the bank EVP, I offered up the best proposal he had seen for this type of test.

"I can do a pen test for free," I told the EVP. "Someone can get in. It may not be me, but there is someone who can do it. Given enough time, all systems can be broken."

The point is, when you're looking to define risk, the pen test doesn't do it. Security isn't introduced believing that we can keep everyone out. Rather, the question should be, "Can we detect and respond before data is stolen or compromised?"

Security Audit

Audits are the third type of assessment. Clients often ask me whether performing an assessment and selling a product are a conflict of interest. If any conflict exists, it's in the context of an audit. Audits are generally defined by the industry as a measure against compliance. They should be performed by someone who is authorized to certify a company as being compliant to a set of standards such as PCI, HIPAA, or GLBA. If a client's system fails, the auditor will provide a report on noncompliant areas. These issues are then addressed by IT or a third party supplier.

Resellers should stay out of the audit business. You want product business that has the potential to become monthly revenue and renewal business, not a one time audit project. Your goal should be to identify more project opportunities and long-term annuity business. Audits won't do that.

The bank EVP was familiar with audits, but I assured him that this was not what his company needed at this moment. What he did need was a measure of risk, and a roadmap to secure his data.

Risk Assessment

While many reports are called risk assessments, few offer any measurement of risk (the measure of impact versus the likelihood something bad will happen.) Certainly, there are more complete definitions that take into consideration business impact (quantitative and qualitative measurements of downtime and disruption), annual rates of expectancy, and other risk-related factors, but let's keep this simple. The goal here is not to build a practice around security assessments, but to build your security program. The risk-assessment process creates the justification required to move your program forward.

Rather than delivering a heavyweight document and charging by the pound, I hope to deliver something fairly simple. It should be a relevant document that helps asset owners understand where they are at risk, which threats matters most, and where to apply their dollars toward the security needed for their business requirements.

A risk assessment is simply a measure of Impact vs. Likelihood. It measures the impact of an issue, and the likelihood that issue will actually occur. While this deliverable is simple to look at, it's the intelligence behind it that makes it unique. In the end, the successful assessment report will find what is needed and convert to new project business. So let's take a look at how that actually happens.

CHAPTER TWENTYONE

Assessments That Convert

> Only about 20% of the assessments I see convert to remediation projects or managed services. Something's wrong. Almost 100% of the time these assessments report critical issues – why don't they convert?

The Assessment Must Convert To Future Business

At the end of the day, assessments are really about conversion. Consider just about any of your clients. Are they secure? The truth is, anyone of them could be compromised. If they are not currently under attack, chances are they will be. Your job is to discover how much risk they actually have and report that to their leaders in a language they understand.

Going back to our doctor examination example, if the doctor detects something that might be cancerous in you, his job is to let you know. If he buries that in a 200 page report that you never read, you'll go untreated. Thirty days go by and you're on your death bed. Now it's too late. Whose fault is this? It's the doctors!

The assessment deliverable must measure risk, but it must also lead to action. Conversion means, the company sees the risk, understands it, and is able to make a responsible decision knowing all of the facts. It might be that they choose to not take action, but that's their choice. But it must be made with the proper intelligence.

When performed correctly, the risk assessment provides senior management with data that has been collected and turned into actionable intelligence. A case has been made to move them to action. In most cases, those with liability will take action if they really understand what is at stake.

Three Things the Board Needs in Order To Make a Decision

In a typical two day board meeting, the agenda will call for about thirty minutes of discussion on security. What are they looking for?

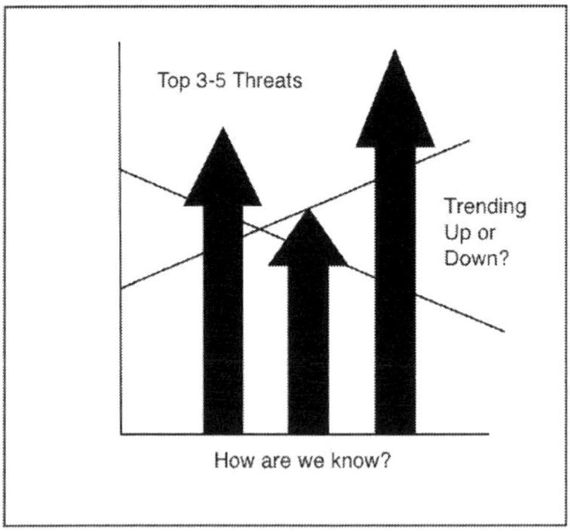

Figure: Impact vs. Likelihood For Board Members

I've stated this a couple of times, but here it is again – you see it's always the same thing. Learn to deliver this and your executive level meetings will be much easier to conduct.

1. **Top 5 to 7 threats**. What are the 5 to 7 most relevant and destructive issues this company is facing at this time. They're most concerned about things like data, applications, customer retention, legal liability, etc.

2. **Are we trending up or down?** Here, the board wants to know if things are getting better or worse. Given the current business initiatives, politics, partnerships, upcoming announcements, etc., is our company's situation becoming more or less risky?

3. **How are we managing to it?** What is the plan to improve, and how are we measuring our progress?

Asset Focused: The Secret to Justification

In a recent sales call with one of my Mastery Group Clients, we were faced with a competitive opportunity to perform a risk assessment. The client was really looking for a vulnerability assessment, but I was convinced he didn't really know what he needed. After all, he was the IT Director, not an Asset Owner.

The meeting opened with him articulating his needs and giving us some background on his company – a company my client had never done business with. My role in the meeting was to coach my client on how to position a risk assessment and how to get to the asset owners quickly.

When it was our turn to talk, instead of opening the floor with the obvious sales 101 questions, I asked the director if he really understood what his board was looking for. From his response I could tell he didn't. And why would he? Few IT directors are ever given the privilege of sitting in on a board meeting or meeting with the C-Levels to discuss these things.

Our job as a sales and consulting team is to help this person get his company the things they need. Getting up at the white board I drew for him a simple IMPACT vs. LIKELIHOOD graph, and began to explain what board members are looking for. If he is going to be successful, he will deliver the same sort of thing to his management, the CIO.

I can already imagine the other proposals coming back. From the dozens of Making Money w/ Security Workshops I've conducted over the past ten years, I know what consulting companies are delivering in their risk reports. And as I've described, they do little to justify action. Only about 20% of them actually lead to change. Instead of heading down the traditional path of assessing networks and systems, it is best to start with the key assets, the thing that is actually at risk.

Here's a Simple Formula to Follow:

1. **Work with Business Leaders to Discover the Assets.** Remember Question 1: "What are you trying to protect?" This question was created to move the conversation away from products and toward assets. **This conversation begins with an asset owner, not technical people.** This assessment starts by identifying the company's most important applications (and data), then moves to assess the risk, and finally delivers results. The report must be written specifically with assets in mind and addressed back to the asset owners. Note: The supporting data can be delivered to the custodians in the form of an appendix. (I provide significant details on how to conduct these assessments in my Security Sales Mastery Program.) This is an excellent

resource for retooling any sales team for executive level security sales.

2. **Work with Power Users to Discover Workflow.** Traditional security assessments focus on perimeter issues, inside and outside security controls, or perhaps the entire enterprise. This approach may work for certain applications, but not for what I propose here. With the key data assets in mind, we should now move to the people who actually create and use the data. The question is, how do they create data, how does it get used, where does it get transmitted, and who interacts with it along the way. The users and department heads over these systems will understand better than anyone, just how important this is, even if they don't understand the technology.

3. **Consider the Entire System.** By entire system, I mean the servers, networks, and connectivity associated with a particular set of assets—something tightly defined that can be accomplished in a short amount of time. We'll consider the entire lifecycle of the data from it's creation to its archival or deletion, and what happens to it along the way. Trusted systems, all points of access, policies, procedures, and anything that may affect assets on a given system are relevant. I'm not saying you must assess the entire organization; rather, take some of the key systems and address all relevant aspects.

4. **Conduct an Internal Review**. After collecting data from the leadership team and meeting with power users it's time to review and predict. There are numerous issues with every system, so relevancy is important. When you have a health exam, you don't want a list of every potential issue or a test for every disease known to mankind. Rather, you

want to know if you face any immediate dangers. Banks, pharmaceutical companies, and manufacturers face different threats. The purpose of this meeting is to work with your technical team to predict where their big holes are if IT hasn't done their job. For instance, if they have a large group of people working at home, or this department travels frequently, what relevant security risks exist in the way they access and handle data?

5. **The IT Walk-Through.** With your internal review in hand, it's time to go back and walk through their data center. Knowing that loan officers use email to work with their clients, does IT have systems in place to make sure account numbers are not being sent out? Or, if the end-users tend to do a lot from home systems, what would happen if a home system were compromised? Would the hacker be able to access company systems through an established VPN connection? These are simple examples, but all too common.

6. **Collect the Evidence.** At some point it is helpful to collect data to prove what you predict to be true. This is not always necessary, particularly in the SMB market, or in a complementary assessment. Like the doctor performing the basic blood test, all you need is evidence that demands further investigation.

7. **The "So What?" Test.** It's almost time to write, but first, there's what I call, "The So What? Test" This is where you and your team review the findings and ask the question, "So What?" over and over until your technical people become annoyed. Too often, the report will be written using phrases such as, "This open port could lead to a compromise with the XYZ Trojan." This is a meaningless

statement. We need business impact on this report. Who can get to what, and how likely is it that they will in the next 6 to 12 months?

8. **Deliver Measurable Risk**. Finally, the Impact vs. Likelihood graph can be created. Using the diagram I've provided in this book, your team must come up with a picture of impact and likelihood. The key systems are listed along the X-Axis in priority order. I like to use a scale of 1 to 10, so it's more like a histogram than a linear scale. And each has an associated measure of likelihood.

9. **Upselling a Continuous Process**. This may be the most important point on this list. Selling a one-time assessment raises awareness, but quarterly updates allow you to manage the remediation process. Selling the client on doing the baseline and then adding a quarterly update (a brief walkthrough) allows you to review new projects, system changes, and future plans to identify issues and concerns. At the same time, as an advisor, you have the opportunity to remind clients of the potential dangers and help them plan and purchase the roadmap you're laying out. Without this last step, you will likely lose your momentum with this account.

Assessments Justify Projects

Risk assessments are performed by companies that specialize in information security. Frequently they are sold as an unbiased look at how secure a given company's systems are. Many people have asked me how to overcome objections to a single company performing this assessment, only to be followed by proposals to sell products and remediation services or managed services. Can one company do it all?

The answer is an emphatic yes. Security boutique companies will use this unbiased line to make the sale, and it is fair to do so. These companies depend on their security expertise and methodology to close business; it's part of their sales strategy. This is no different than the "point product" strategy that brings security decisions and product evaluations down to a feature/function battle.

Consider the alarm salesperson. He comes to your home, walks through your halls, garage, and around the back of the house; and begins pointing out where the holes are. He shows you how easy it is to break in, basically performing a free assessment. If he is really good at what he does, he will convince you that your home is unsafe. He has essentially become your trusted advisor. The sale is made by showing you how the impact can be avoided by reducing the likelihood of an attack or intrusion.

At this point, the salesperson becomes your consultant and begins to design your security system. He takes the data from the free assessment, and he looks at the location of your doors, windows and other points of entry. He reviews your home's construction, location, neighborhood, lighting, and visibility to other homes. From there he will come up with a design consisting of door and window sensors, glass break monitors, and motion detection. For higher-end implementations, he may toss in video surveillance and, in the end, may sell you a managed services program (24/7 monitoring, with no guarantees).

Notice that by performing the assessment himself, he moves from being a sales person to becoming your advisor. His proposal is more of a prescription and less of a product pitch. If you want a secure home, here is what you will do.

It would be rare to hire an outside firm with no security products to design this system. You look to the manufacturer or value-added reseller to understand the risks, what products to use, and then to perform the installation. An assessment is not an audit, in this case, but a process that takes the client from conception to implementation, and then to a managed service program. I cannot think of one assessment I've sold, with this concept in mind, that hasn't led to product sales.

The Deliverable: The Key to Justification

The critical factor in everything I've discussed is the deliverable. Once you're established as the consultant who performs the assessment, the relationship must remain at the asset owner level. This is rare in my experience, but sales people must become a central player in the assessment process. This is not technology, it's business acumen. This is your opportunity to gain access to almost anyone in the organization without your sales hat on.

Following the initial executive-level meetings, the technical presales person will perform the information-gathering at the technical levels. The internal analysis will involve your sales and technical people, and the deliverables will be presented at the Asset Owner level by sales. The technical assessment materials may then be provided by the presales or billable technical team.

Concurrently, you are working with your higher-level consultants at the business level to understand the applications, data value, and impact vs. likelihood of things going bad. Your primary deliverable is written with the Asset Owner and business executive in mind. I recommend using charts, pictures, and bullet points to communicate clearly what the client must do to reduce exposure.

Formal presentations should be used to explain what you found. Recommend actionable steps based on impact numbers or weightings, justifying your recommendations with your likelihood numbers. A roadmap is used to paint a picture of what could be and how the enterprise may be extended to new markets where computing is unsafe.

The Immediate Sale Starts Here

Most companies will not purchase large security remediation projects the day after an assessment. They conduct these projects with planning in mind. However, sales approached from the angle taken in this book target new opportunities and unbudgeted initiatives. The idea is to get the client to see something for which he isn't already creating RFPs for. Something urgent.

If someone were to come by your home with evidence of a suspected pipe break under your house, you might at least let them check. If, during their assessment, they were to produce more concrete evidence, would you wait a few weeks on a quote? No! You would want it addressed immediately. This is how the assessment should be presented. Find the urgent things, frame them up with the business critical systems you've observed, and help your Asset Owner level clients see the urgency. For instance, if there is a bot present, don't call it a virus. Bots come from an outsider who has gained access to internal systems, installed unauthorized software, and who now has the potential to access data. It is in fact, a Trojan Horse. Remember, the asset owner will see this as urgent. But they need someone to explain it to them in business language.

Subscription Programs

The subscription is the final factor in selling your program—a critical part of driving the roadmap.

The subscription gives you control over future project initiatives. Every month/quarter, you're back in front of the managers, reviewing new projects and system changes that affect their overall security architecture and represent new levels of risk. At the same time, you are reminding them of the exposure they already have, given no remediation efforts.

This is not a time to sell hard, but to continually position your company as a trusted advisor. Done right, you should find yourself invited to planning sessions, company meetings, and opportunities to present your findings and recommendations to other executives (and, potentially, board members).

Each quarter, you should update what you have and expand your view into the client's computing environment. Every project, system change, or application addition or enhancement is potentially an increase in the existing project's scope. Updates represent reminders of the progress toward remediation, while scope expansions introduce you to new projects that may provide opportunities for other company offerings. Of course, scope changes should also represent fee changes.

The bottom line: Use the subscription process to expand your presence, deliver greater value, and position your company as the go-to provider for maintaining data availability, confidentiality, and integrity on any part of the client's infrastructure. This is not a pure security product sale; it touches every aspect of creating, using, transmitting, storing, archiving, and disposing of mission-critical data.

A Simple Upsell

Here's a simple way to upsell the assessment as a subscription.

Price out your assessment (assuming it's fee based). Assessment prices vary considerably, so price this on the high side of what you would normally do, yet within range of what it's true value is.

Perform one day visits. Specify your subscription as an update to the existing scope to be done in one day. Since the deliverable is already written, updating the existing scope should be pretty easy. Use this time to discover unremediated findings from the original scope, as well as new threats that might have come about as a result of advancements in hacker tools or new company initiatives. Discover any new plans and how they might affect your client's future security posture.

This service is a win/win. Your client is getting the updates they need while you are controlling the scorecard for the ongoing security initiatives. This puts you first in line for any future security issues, as well as giving you insight into new projects and initiatives involving technology.

This is a simple strategy I used back in the early 2000s while selling security assessments. I quoted this same program on every assessment I proposed. Not once was it rejected or cut from an assessment we won.

Delivering Risk to The Right Audience Leads to Business Every Time

When do you bring the proposal? Most sales start with the influencer, but influencers are not liable for risk. Realistically, the IT manager or IT personnel are the folks who are willing to take the meetings, and you have to start somewhere. This is not necessarily bad, but it needs to be approached correctly. For instance, if a lead comes in from a partner, marketing event, or trade show, it is the IT custodian who will look at available technology, seek education, and request free evaluation equipment. But security, as I've previously indicated, is not sold to IT or security people, but to the person with liability; the Asset Owner.

The assessments I am talking about don't start at the IT level. So if your IT contact is asking, don't work on closing until you work on moving up. I provide an extensive section on the moving-up process in my book, *From Vendor to Adviser*. I highly recommend reading Chapter 6 – Moving Up Strategies, before proceeding.

In Chapter 6 of *From Vendor to Adviser*, I explain how to work the influencer meeting and how to move up from there. Influencer meetings are important, but remember they can't make a decision.

They don't want to admit that they are, in fact, powerless.

As the salesperson, you're looking for direction. You need to know if a lead is worth pursuing, and you want your prospect to provide some indication of the next step. What do you do?

You Need An Asset Owner to Move Forward

The answer should be obvious: You need to find the asset owner. Remember what I said earlier, "Forget about products, focus on the assets. Then, find the asset owner." The person you are talking to can likely help you get there, but convincing him to do this requires some finesse. You can't force this individual to admit he has no power. Study the four meeting model in *From Vendor to Advisor* and you'll have the access you need. As you make your move upward, you'll want to make sure you understand the real needs and have a message to move them toward an agreed upon vision. Let's look now at the important need every one of your clients has and how to move them forward.

CHAPTER TWENTYTWO

No One Has It Covered

> No matter how many companies get hacked, the same issues keep coming up. Some are more powerful than others when it comes to justification.

In the Fifth Discipline, Peter Senge explains that people will die for a vision they really believe in. When they understand current realities, see the possibilities of what could be, and believe in their advisors' ability to take them there, they'll make the journey.

Persuasion: "Guiding vital truths around others' mental roadblocks." (Character Training Institute)

Sales are made using the justification and guidance you provide through the assessment process described in this book. Once you have justification, the sale can be made. It's the art of persuasion that allows you to show buyers the truth in ways that allow them to make intelligent buying decisions.

Everything starts with a new understanding of the risks involved in running a business dependent on mission-critical assets. The prospect agrees threats are changing. Protection, detection, and response are now all necessary to the security architecture. His current strategy, using "protection alone" to guard his most precious assets, is no longer valid.

Perhaps he has hired you to assess risk. Show him the impact vs. likelihood graph and he'll see it. Then help him prioritize his action plan.

Turning Esoteric Data Into Powerful Sales Artillery – Reading the Assessment

For ten years I have been conducting Security Sales classes. Thousands of security sales and consulting professionals have attended these classes—from product manufacturers, software developers, solution providers, security boutiques, large integrators, and smaller mid-market and SMB solution providers/resellers. On day two, I always ask them where they find their greatest opportunities. Where are the big holes in the average security architecture? It's what I call, The Predictable Message.

Here's The List That Always Comes Out:

Policy. While most companies have a security policy, it's generally meaningless, out of date, and stuck on a shelf somewhere. Employees may have read it when they joined the company, but no one remembers what it says. And there is no record of them having actually read it and signed off on it. In most cases, the company's policy lacks supporting standards and procedures. Across the board, policies lack enforcement, reducing them to a set of guidelines. They don't necessarily limit liability or drive architecture, as they're designed to do. Bottom line, they are simply a checkmark for the compliance officer and do little to actually secure data.

Segmentation. Internal networks are treated as one big trusted family. Regardless of division lines companies have failed to provide segmentation among divisions requiring different degrees of security. This was the case with Target. As a result, hackers were able to make there way in through a third-party connection used by Target's HVAC contractor. Segmentation is basic, and necessary, yet often disregarded.

Web Applications. Web applications are particularly deficient when it comes to security. While there are application testing tools available, as well as application-specific firewalls, many companies aren't using them. I've had conversations with third-party application developers who say it's just too costly and time-consuming to put security into the application. They recommend that clients secure data using firewalls and other security devices. This is unbelievable and unacceptable.

IP-Telephony. This is another example of an application—one that may perhaps be the creator and transmitter of some of the most critical information in the organization. This is where companies handle mergers and acquisitions, stock trades, employee decisions, changes to key products, new ideas—in short, the future of the organization. Why do so many companies assume this is a safe place to create and transmit highly sensitive information?

Server and Operating System Security. Large servers are connected to web applications, allowing third-party processing, customers, internal users, external users, and anyone else to create or interact with data. Assessments have shown system security is generally weak, granting users complete access (including create, read, write and deletion rights) to key data. User IDs often remain active after employees are gone. As jobs change and needs evolve, users' access rights often are out of step with their needs. Administrators often create *back doors* or trusted relationships among systems to ease their burden, but wind up creating significant weaknesses in the security architecture. This is done far more often than executives believe, and most often without any approval.

Remote Access. Remote access always seems to be a problem. With just about every company engaged in BYOD (Bring Your Own Device) projects, and demanding access to mission-critical data from just about anywhere, data security is nearly impossible to manage without some kind of third party assistance. Systems used at home by young people and parents for chatting, blogging, shopping, and often connected through peer-to-peer networks for gaming and illegal music/video exchanges, are then used to access corporate systems. Mobile devices are accessing these same systems from airports, hotels, coffee shops and public hotspots without any concern for privacy. Simple passwords, POP3 mail protocols, webmail, and instant-messaging applications are used to transmit highly sensitive information in the clear. Most business users have no idea how easy it is to grab information by exploiting social media and phone applications.

Disaster Recovery and Back Ups. This one is unbelievable given all the press on lost data. Yet companies still fail to back up their data. I recently had a client involved in a complementary assessment where they discovered a mission critical server backing up to itself. The larger companies tend to have disaster recovery and business continuity plans in place, but they are often inadequate and untested. I was working with a major manufacturing firm in N.C. a few years ago. It appeared to us that their tape backup system was on its way out and the current tape set didn't look right. We recommended a change, but the cost scared them away. Three days later their disk crashed. The resulting cost was three days of three shifts downtime, plus a thirty-thousand dollar recovery bill. Looking back, I realize we were dealing at the wrong level in this account, and had not delivered a powerful enough value proposition to the right people. This is a sales problem.

Wireless. Despite the endless stories about war driving, companies have not upgraded their wireless networks to higher standards of encryption. However, cybercriminals have also discovered that many home networks are not encrypted at all. With today's Internet searching capabilities it's not hard to find out where people live and attack businesses from an executive's home network.

Partners, Guests and Contractors. While many companies have managed to secure the perimeter, back-door connections are often created to allow partners to share applications. This was Target's problem. With the growth of "The Internet of Things," everything is connected, and third-party companies with weak security policies have access. In a recent Wall Street Journal article, a writer stated that tens of thousands of U.S. Government contractors were granted high-level access while waiting on security clearance approval. We have a long list of data leaks on record associated with government contractors who should not have been trusted – Edward Snowden is just one example (Reference the 2013 NSA leaks.)

The Most Powerful Finding Ever

There's no end to the number of issues you'll find in the average assessment, but the one most often overlooked is MALWARE! Remember, it is urgent!

Real-Life Situations

My own findings support the problems I've just identified. I recently received payment from a major global company through the Internet. I was sitting in an airport, accessing a plain-text email account. One of my messages contained a client's credit card, security code and expiration date.

In another recent case one of my clients was assessing a company's security. There email gateway had been compromised and they were being used to route spam all over the world.

One of my larger technology manufacturing clients calls on a major software developer that processes accounting data for small companies throughout the United States. A recent firewall issue threatened to shut down his software application. During a particularly busy time of year, one of the supporting integration firms actually recommended that they pull out the firewalls temporarily and use access control lists until the firewall problem could be solved. It's been more than a month since they implemented this temporary fix—and these accounts hold all kinds of information that could be used by cyber-thieves to create new identities or apply for loans, among other risks.

Another client was donating PCs to charity without deleting data. He was erasing the disks, but studies show it's relatively easy to recover data from an erased disk.

While working with a regional bank, I discovered its primary banking applications running on an AS/400 provided complete access to third-party processing companies. They had rights to not only read information, but to change or delete it. This bank also transmits account information across the Internet as part of its loan approval process—clearly a violation of GLBA.

I could go on, but you get my point. Security is weak, and much of the problem can be fixed without getting into highly technical details. Security issues are not new. The IT people have limited liability and are not clearly communicating the risks to company leadership. With this gap in knowledge and understanding, most of the companies you are dealing with have very poor security in place. This is more than a product sale.

CHAPTER TWENTYTHREE

Re-Engineering The Product Sale

> Point product sales don't secure anything. They also don't produce much In the way of profit. Basically they are a waste of time. Turn your product quotes into projects and you'll be on your way to advising.

The Product List

When an assessment uncovers the kinds of issues I've just discussed, your first inclination may be to start listing products. Take a look at the list of products you sell. There are likely many, some of which overlap; some more expensive; and some more relevant than others. You shouldn't view it as a product list, but as a component list.

My friend purchases and restores historical homes. When I first entered the last home he purchased—a 100-year-old house in

South Carolina—I was amazed at the amount of work he faced. One of the obvious issues was the electrical systems. With holes in the walls and missing light fixtures, you could see the wiring wouldn't meet state codes. I imagined what would happen if someone were standing in a puddle of water and turned on a faulty appliance—a disaster waiting to happen.

If I were an electrician, my first thought would be to assess the situation—to walk through, crawl through and inspect every part of the system. Going back to my truck, I would have numerous components to choose from to create a safe living environment.

You should view your component list in the same way. Don't call them solutions. They're not! Don't think of them as products to sell either. Components are the right idea. They give you the idea that products/integration, policies, and education are all required to create a safe computing environment. In fact, all nine boxes of the coverage model should be considered as one seamless system or security architecture.

Remote-Access Example

We've all sold VPNs. Assume a prospect comes to you and asks you to sell one. What's your response? You might ask how many ports are needed, how many users will use the system, and which applications the client is planning to support. These questions will lead you right back to IT— not the place we want to start.

Try another approach. Ask: "What are you trying to protect?" Looking at the VPN solution, we can assume there's a need to access key systems remotely. But this can actually be done without the aid of a VPN. The VPN was introduced to provide some level of security. What does the VPN actually provide? Your first thought may be secure remote access, but does it really do this? Your second answer may be encryption of data. This answer is correct, but how secure is it?

The fact is, encrypting data may make systems less secure. Of course, I'm exaggerating a bit to make my point. But because data cannot be seen, whatever is happening on an end-node is passing through the perimeter—perhaps to a DMZ area on the network, but through the firewall, without the ability to see what's coming in.

The solution is to add something to this picture. After I ask, "What are you trying to protect?", I have the information I need to start designing a more secure way to access data remotely. I may add some way to authenticate users with two-factor authentication.

Secondly, I should add some way to ensure their devices have the right patches, are running the latest software versions, and meet company standards. I can do this with some type of network access control server (NAC.)

It would be helpful to have some level of intrusion-prevention software running at the perimeter, ensuring malicious traffic doesn't enter the corporation's trusted network. And don't forget a way to monitor activity: when users come in, who they are, what they do, and when they leave. Accountability is important here – this is the essence of data leakage. Is there real time monitoring and alerting, as well as an audit trail?

At the end-node, the operating system must be protected from all forms of malware, spyware, and misuse. Several applications may be required to do this, and the prospect may have much of this in place. It is the salesperson's job, regardless of whether he sells these products, to recommend using them.

Wireless Application

With the remote access example, you will recommend some way to keep the end-node safe from malware and remote-control attacks by using antivirus, anti-spyware, and perhaps some form of intrusion-prevention software. Your corporate network assessed the end-node's condition before allowing a connection to be established, you then checked with an access control server to ensure the user was authorized to come in. You determined the restrictions that should be applied to each session. You ensured the user was, in fact, who he claimed to be by using strong authentication. Finally, you provided encryption and some means of centrally managing this activity.

Moving to a wireless application, what would have to change? If you guessed nothing, you're right. It's the same scenario. The end user must be clean, authenticated, authorized, and permitted. Once connected, he must be monitored.

In fact, regardless of where this connection occurs (internal or external, wireless, partner, consultant, guest, or other,) the same steps are required. Encryption may not be required in some instances, and a simple password may work for some internal users. But in general, you should recommend these basic safety controls if the user is going to achieve secure remote access or secure access of any kind.

Systems and Storage

You may have opportunities with servers, storage, and end-user devices. Each concept should be applied to the OS, application, and database. Again, it's the same scenario of ensuring a clean system, authentication, authorization, and event correlation. Encryption is applied to transmission, storage, and archival.

In each case, the three pillars of security are applied: confidentiality, integrity, and availability of the system and its data. In the network case, single points of failure are eliminated. In the systems and storage area, the same is true, with the added function of ensuring proper backups and restore capability.

If you have sold in the systems arena for any length of time, you should recognize that tapes often fail, and system failures often take far longer than the average four-hour response time to be placed back in full service. This is why Symantec bought Veritas in 2005. In its quest to secure data, operating systems, and applications, it needed the capability to back up data and create a highly available configuration.

Voice Applications

Voice over IP is a popular networking application. Whenever I lead a workshop, I run into companies focused on this technology. Back when I wrote the first edition of the House & the Cloud, I predicted that VoIP resellers would be selling commodity products within a few years. People actually got mad at me in some of my workshops. At a recent Westcon Security Conference, where I was delivering the keynote address on creating an effective security value proposition, one of the VPs announced from the stage that VoIP sales were on the decline. How do resellers recover? Security is the answer.

Several features make VoIP attractive, including the managed services offerings built around it. But notice that by focusing on the security aspects, value differentiation still stands. Commodity products can still represent a strong business when the underlying sale is made on security.

When people pick up the phone, they are convinced their conversations are off the record. This is also true with email correspondence despite the numerous warnings over the years. I am amazed at how many politicians have been caught in affairs and illegal activities simply because they didn't understand the concept of digital assets and log files.

It's not that traditional analog voice applications couldn't be taped or recorded; they could and sometimes were. But the tools available today for network-hacking allow intruders to easily record voice along with data. And because we know bots and other malicious software products are being used across all infrastructure to steal information, we can be sure people are tapping into VoIP.

Companies that could be securing their voice are not. People who sell voice are not educating consumers on its risks in an effort to keep the sale moving. But this is a disservice to the customer and a missed opportunity to set yourself apart. It's easy to record voice on a network—to sit between two executive callers with a PC and capture information discussed regarding future mergers, big sales opportunities, coming layoffs, or the latest product roadmaps.

Some of the simplest steps aren't being taken. Newer switch and router technologies are designed for voice to improve quality and give administrators the necessary security to keep an eye on their networks. The use of simple logging tools, as well as centralized correlation and alerting, can go a long way toward creating a secure computing environment. Again, a lot of these things are not the new state-of-the-art devices. It's the simple stuff that is killing these companies. The technology used has been around for a long time, but simple steps of network segmentation are not being used.

Greater security can be achieved, but it takes thought and due care. It requires that companies view security as a way of detecting an intrusion with a well thought out response plan; verses a firewall that will keep people out.

CHAPTER TWENTYFOUR

New Technologies Changing the Face of Security:

> Cloud, BYOD, Data Analytics and Big Data, and Collaboration Technologies like Google+ are game changers. They are transforming the way we do business; security needs to change too.

Disruptive technologies are changing the face of security. Everything I've mentioned is basic. It's been around for years. Yet, the basic steps of securing these devices is still pathetic in many cases. But the face of security is changing. The concept of perimeter security is largely gone with the advent of mobility. Cloud, Big Data, BYOD, and Social Business change everything.

Cloud Computing

Cloud means a lot of things, but here I am talking about hosted storage and applications. Whether Evernote (Evernote.com) is being used by a single person to store work documents, Amazon to provide cloud storage, or an application like ZipCloud that backs up my data to the cloud, the data is no longer in the data center.

Call it insecure, or whatever you want, cloud-apps are here to stay. It's like instant messaging was years ago. Companies have tried to stop it, but they can't. In a recent Wall Street Journal report, IT support teams were asked how many cloud applications their companies where using. They guessed about 150. One hundred fifty applications in a single company! But get this; the same study was done at the departmental level, giving answers closer to 350. IT has no idea who is using what cloud application. Meanwhile, departments, in an effort to get their work done, are quickly migrating to whatever cloud application looks helpful, without IT's involvement.

In general, I believe cloud security is a gamble, however I also see that small and medium businesses are not going to do the right thing when it comes to security, nor can they afford it. This makes cloud the right choice. I am using cloud despite my earlier comments, to store data, distribute documents, host email, and for CRM (Infusionsoft.com). I also back up to the cloud and shop online all the time. However, I also keep a close eye on credit card statements and credit reports.

Cloud is a major migration path for companies right now. The best thing for technology providers to do is embrace it. Meanwhile, they should be searching out the most secure practices and safeguards to support this move.

App Stores and BYOD

Closely related to cloud is the app store. The end-user experience is becoming of great importance. CIOs and CISOs who inhibit production will soon find themselves out on the street seeking new employment. The new mindset is an app mindset. Pull out your smartphone, search for an app that does something you need, and download it. It should be a matter of seconds before you're in production.

Having to wait brings aggravation and frustration. This same mindset carries over to IT. End-users are not willing to wait on testing, and they're not willing to use corporate issued devices. Today people live their lives on their computer. They shop, bank, entertain, talk on the phone, and work, all on their laptop and tablet. They even control their home security, HVAC, and monitor daycare from their phones and laptops. While there are enterprise applications to handle some of this, the midsize and SMB companies will not have it. They are turning to iTunes, Dropbox or Google Drives, and App stores for their business applications. The question remains, how can you best support your clients' security given they will be doing this?

Social Business and Social Media

Studies show that office workers spend an average of 4 hours per day on social media sites and shopping. Of course this is a waste of time and in fact stealing from the company, but it also opens up many holes for hackers. People don't think twice about interacting with people they don't know online.

Remember the woman who successfully convinced 73% of the men in a Manhattan based financial firm to give up highly sensitive information. And the 13% who handed over passwords!

Social media has completely changed the face of privacy. If people are willing to send nude photos of themselves over the Internet. What else will they send?

CHAPTER TWENTYFIVE

The Key to Managed Services:

Security and risk mitigation will bring more profitable managed services deals, strengthen your existing programs, and differentiate you from the competition.

By Steve Rutkovitz & Ben Schmerler

Choice Technologies, Inc.

Managed services is largely a security sale. The principles David illustrates in this book speak to the experiences we have had at Choice Technologies. Our business has evolved significantly over the past several years, moving from an SMB VAR to a full Managed Security Services company; a far more profitable business model.

In this chapter I'd like to discuss how the environment for selling Managed Services has changed. I'll explain how you as a salesperson can leverage these changes to produce results in the form of increased sales, better client retention, and greater differentiation. I'll review how we changed our product mix to sell services that spoke more to our clients concerns regarding risk and security management, and I will also discuss strategies for making sure that your company is properly equipped to provide and sell these services. My hope is you will walk away with a strategy to shorten sales cycles, produce higher margin business on top of your existing managed services offerings, and increase the long-term value of the services you provide to your clients. In addition, you'll find that by adding security to your managed offerings you'll be out in front of your clients more, driving project based sales that are like the gravy on top of your annuity based revenue.

Most of our clients are medical doctors, attorneys, accountants, and financial services professionals. We also work with many related businesses that touch our professional services clients in some way through a partnership or third party processing function. All of them face similar scrutiny when it comes to their IT security. After investing several years in researching these businesses, we have finally created a Managed Security offering that not only offers tremendous business potential for our company, but also is now being resold through other resellers who are wanting to offer this type of value without making the investment in time and money to build it.

Why, If You Don't Make This Change, You May Be Out Of Business

The market for managed services has changed. When I first started at Choice, our competitive advantage was our knowledge and expertise. We were experts at configuring and supporting complicated computer and networking equipment. As a result, we were able to charge a premium for our services and faced less competition. Our clients needed our expertise in order to implement Electronic Medical Records systems, Practice

Management Systems, as well as the basic security and backup products used to prevent data loss and downtime.

The market has changed. The professionals we sell to no longer need high-end expertise to create a digital workplace. Mobile devices such as smartphones and tablets require only a few presses of a button and their apps install. Even backup technology and firewall appliances are easy to set up these days. And to make things even more simplified, many of these services and systems are now provided and managed by cable companies and product vendors. Bottom line, they no longer require our technical expertise for these services. Our competitive advantage has mostly disappeared with the exception of specialized, one-off projects.

But as technology commoditizes, new opportunities are appearing. Turn on any news channel. It seems like every day there is a story about a major corporation being hacked. Just this year Target, Home Depot, and JP Morgan have lost more than 200 million customer records combined. The organizations I work with simply cannot afford to deal with these kinds of security concerns. It's over their heads and extremely intimidating for people who were educated and trained to practice medicine or law to have to deal with data security.

So while our clients are downloading apps and plugging in appliances, they are asking for something new – information. For example, how do they know that people aren't trying to break into their network? How can they be sure that their data is being backed up properly? What if a fire or flood were to wipe out their building? Could they recover? And what about their employees? Are they taking the security and workflow policies of the organization seriously? If someone does the wrong thing can it be identified and addressed before damage occurs? Will the business leaders be able to take corrective action before there are major legal or financial consequences? Notice that none of these questions have anything to do with our ability to configure a product. They speak more to risk management; they're business issues that require technical expertise

How Does A Reseller Evolve And Move Upstream?

Over time our sales cycles began slowing down. Before long we were facing significant price pressures on both product resale and implementation services. Fortunately for us, we had built up a strong portfolio of Managed Services clients who appreciated our expertise in IT Management and Security. So as the market began to shift, our medical clients came to us with a new set of needs. They were being asked to comply with new "Meaningful Use" requirements set by the federal government; a requirement if they were to be reimbursed for the investments they were making in EMR software. Some of these EMR investments totaled in the hundreds of thousands of dollars. And if a data breach were to occur, not only would their reputation be ruined by the media; they would likely end up paying huge fines to the government, and in some cases incur criminal prosecution. We were in the right place at the right time, but our offering had to mature.

This explains why our company had to change. If we wanted to move upstream, we needed a Managed Services offering that addressed and minimized these risks. Moving forward, every product we offer our clients has to either provide extra value in terms of productivity/efficiency or reduce the risk of loss, theft, or misuse. Productivity is a nice sell, but there are limitations to what you can offer and actually prove in terms of ROI. For example, if you are selling a hosted Exchange solution to replace a legacy mail server, most people look at the cost over the life of both solutions and make a purely economic decision. It's a commodity offering that we will continue to provide as part of our comprehensive offer. But the truth is that most of our clients aren't working with us for this type of solution. They are working with us because we understand that they have valuable assets in the form of data and IT resources and they need them managed and protected. Offering hosted Exchange, servers, switches, or any commoditized product as part of our Managed Services solution gives our clients one place to shop. But it's those higher-end managed security offerings that create unique value. And if a client has a less costly way to buy commoditized IT product, we recommend they buy it there and we'll take on the installation and management of it. What's the point in arguing about a few margin points? The real value, and therefore money, is recurring every month as part of a healthy Managed Services agreement.

When our team meets with a new prospect to share our value proposition, we take time to identify their pain points. Almost always their pain is some kind of risk. Maybe it's the risk of their systems going down, or it might be the fear of loss or misuse. Often the prospect is overwhelmed. They are unable to make a wise decision on the proper investments; they're locked up with too many decisions and not enough understanding. Or maybe they just don't know what their risks are and can't accurately quantify what kind of investment to make. Whatever it is, they are worried about something and need counsel. These people are too busy with their business to be dealing with complex computer issues.

The first step is often an assessment; a way to quantify risk which David has already defined as a measure of impact vs. likelihood. Sometimes these assessments are basic. In the basic assessment we simply want to understand what kind of environment their IT operates in. In this case we are looking to come up with a series of recommendations which are really proposals for Managed Services or projects. Other times there's a need to offer a more comprehensive assessment. In this case we focus on the more complex issues. We might be examining internal workflows or policies to see how the end users actually use technology. Once again, this is a much different approach than the typical firewall installation sale. It puts us in a unique position on the business side, out of reach of our competition. And depending on how comprehensive these assessments are, we may or may not charge for our initial consultation.

If the future VAR selling IT services is to survive, and if you as a salesperson are going to increase your business, it's important that you create a menu of products that can be bundled together and sold as a program; an annuity business. This approach will increase both the health of your business as well as your ability to meet the true needs of your clients. Future clients are not going to pay high fees just to get commodity products installed. And IT support services, such as block time, are notoriously difficult to sell without competing on price. And as VARs continue to roll up into large global integrators these larger commodity VARs will offer cheaper, but impersonal Help Desk services.

Our approach is to sell against low price competitors by focusing on high quality service with a local company. Unfortunately that message does not always resonate in the way we would like it to. Even though this type of service is better, the SMB market is not willing to spend more for it. The future VAR message has to change. The place where they really will need that local expertise is in the area of security and risk management.

The security managed services message differentiates. It leads to more sales, more satisfied clients, and a much stronger value proposition. And when your client does actually experience a security event, your quality response will build closer relationships and greater appreciation. The trusted advisor relationship that David speaks to earlier in the book is what we are talking about here. When you become a trusted advisor you bring education and consultation to the table. Your prospects and clients will invite you to sell to them. For example, when I sell a backup and disaster recovery product, I don't focus on how much it costs per gigabyte.

My sale is about potential real life scenarios that happen (sometimes with real world examples from clients who didn't opt to use my products.) I focus on how our recommendations are built and how effective they will be. When I work with a medical clinic with limited financial resources and tell him that my backup and disaster recovery product can restore their system in a couple hours, the significant monthly recurring cost is not what we talk about. We talk about what risks he will be avoiding by deploying a solution that allows him to sleep well at night. I want him to understand that his practice, which he worked hard to develop and wouldn't want to lose over a hack or server failure, is protected.

Offering A Solution of Protection, Detection, and Remediation

Choice is a little bit larger than we were when I first started, but only by a few employees. So when I say we are security experts, I'm not saying that we personally design and host all of these solutions. Our value to our clients is that we know what to deploy, how to deploy it, where to invest, and where not to invest. That's how you become a trusted advisor. Choice matches the products and services we either provide ourselves or get from a trusted partner to create a comprehensive security and risk mitigation offering.

Choice is an IT management company more than an IT services company. Our early sales focused on the protection aspect of security, and often times today those sales will lead into more comprehensive services. But the clients who appreciate us most, and which are the most profitable to our business, are the ones who want to take a comprehensive managed approach.

Our value now is more in line with educating the asset owners. Sometimes I will appeal to their own expertise because fundamentally they just look at technology as an unknown entity.

That's a good thing. When I meet with a doctor or a wealth manager, I remind them that they are not in business to manage IT. They didn't study this stuff in school and yet they are ultimately responsible for making these decisions. In fact, there are probably a lot of other things they would rather be thinking about. Many of these professionals almost resent technology because of its complexity. In many cases it hinders their real work rather than enabling them.

It's simple. Let me worry about the risks while you focus on your clients or patients. My first meeting with a prospect is always about gathering information. So when I'm setting up a meeting, perhaps via email or on a brief phone call, I let them know exactly what I plan to discuss when I show up. What applications do they rely on the most? Are they committed to those applications or are they thinking about making a change? What is their biggest frustration or concern? On top of these questions, I sometimes challenge them to tell me what they would do in certain situations. For example I might ask them what would happen if their application server went down for a day. I ask them if this type of thing has ever happened before. Of course if they respond that it has, I'll ask them every detail about that experience. They need to remember what's at stake here. I might ask them if they have tested their disaster recovery or backup plan. These are all questions that I think speak to prevention.

But another question I might ask is whether they know if a file was deleted intentionally or unintentionally by an employee. Or how they would tell if someone actually broke into their network and was snooping around. These types of questions go upstream. I believe that detection is the highest value and most compelling proposition to the client or prospect. I use these questions to get my client thinking about security intelligence and the need to know what's going on at any moment. This leads to discussing events and event correlation. A service we provide using Security

Information and Event Management (SIEM) technology.

Our SIEM collects logs from all devices on the network for the purposes of recording, analyzing, and remediating security issues of our clients. These issues are not limited to hacks from the outside, but also reveal employees who knowingly or unknowingly steal or misuse data. If someone is using a PC that is unintentionally giving away data through a bot or other malware, we'll know it and be able to respond. The value of this service to any client is clear. So we want our clients to understand that paying thousands of dollars per month for this type of security intelligence is worth the investment. If we can help stop a breach that leads to a $2.5 million HIPAA fine, which is a likely event (e.g. The Recent Community Health Systems hack resulting in the loss of 4.5 million patient records,) the investment has paid for itself. If Community Health Systems had been using SIEM technology perhaps the fine and other inevitable consequences of this event never would have happened.

My message to clients and prospects is that there is a very good chance they will be attacked or experience some kind of security related emergency in the near future. Whether it's a disaster that makes their data unavailable, or a rogue employee, or a breach where assets are stolen, something will go wrong. Next I help design a solution to prevent this. Our job is to put together a comprehensive plan that outlines all of their risks. It provides a program to reduce their risk to an acceptable level. I'll show them exactly what we can do to detect a breach, and then explain how our team will help them remediate any security issues we discover. We'll use case studies with existing clients that speak to our capability, showing what happens when clients do or do not follow our recommendations. Examples might include anything from a client who had sprinklers mistakenly go off in their data center to identifying a server outage, or a weekend emergency restore. We can't always prevent the incident from happening, but we can often detect and remediate before a major disaster occurs.

The first SIEM our company ever deployed discovered over 5,000 attempted breaches on a single email server in just one day. This reinforced the message that someone is trying to break into their network…we just had to find out who, when, and how they were doing it. With the intelligence we now had, we were able to block the offending IP address and take counter measures to make sure this attempt was stopped. We continue to monitor this client's network, reinforcing our message that detection is essential to the security model. One nice thing about becoming a security expert is that it helps your marketing and prospecting program. Your clients will want to refer you to prospects that will value your security services because they are so grateful that you resolved such an important challenge for them.

How Can Your Company Make the Leap To Managed Security Services ? With Minimal Hassle?

Looking back, we put a ton of effort into our Managed Services program; and then added the Managed Security Services component once our managed program was up and running. The reason I outlined all of the other services we offer is because all of these steps and learning experiences were crucial for us to crack the code on Managed Security.

We had to get into businesses that appreciate what we are offering from a total service standpoint. We needed an understanding of their needs from an industry perspective. And then we had to learn how to create a message that matched our expertise and value to what they needed to hear in order to close a deal. Not only that, we had to mingle in the right crowds. In a sense, this was all market research, even though we were doing it as an exercise in selling and growing our book of business. I would say that even to this day we are still constantly working to refine our messaging regarding our products because data owners are constantly shifting gears and changing their own goals. That's okay, because this kind of refinement speaks to the broader approach of being a trusted advisor. It helps reinforce the message of trust as we strive to improve our products and processes.

As we've grown in our understanding of our clients' needs, we have been forced to move from what I call "Security 1.0" (Basic perimeter protection,) to a Managed Security Services offering, "Security 2.0." This higher level offering not only focuses on basic security protection, but also incorporates the 24/7 monitoring and remediation services that most IT support companies lack. Where we once installed firewalls and antivirus software, the complexity of our clients' operations now demand continuous monitoring and intelligence. Not only are our clients becoming more enticing targets for the bad guys, we also needed a way to create differentiation with a message of compliance and risk management.

First we had to add offsite backup and disaster recovery services, then we had to add server monitoring, and finally SIEM capabilities. Each of these offerings were vetted with our specific clients and industries in mind. We had to figure out if we could sell these products on the value of things like productivity increases or risk mitigation as opposed to price, because as David points out in the previous chapters, you don't want to compete on price as a Managed Services company. There's strength in the message, "I know Carbonite is less expensive, but this is a product I control, manage, and have confidence in. I know it will meet the standards you need for compliance and risk control". If the asset owner doesn't see this, I know they are commoditizing me. Trying to sell higher-end Managed Services to this person will probably lead to similar price-focused discussions; not a sale I am interested in. I'm looking to bring on clients that will appreciate the full scope of services as opposed to a point product sale.

Managed Services are like adding layers to what most people commoditize. That's why we've turned Managed Services into a process. We describe it as Assess, Address, and Maintain. This motto is something we bring to every one of our clients and prospects. It changes to conversation from selling a bunch of products to selling a program. If the prospect buys into the process of Assess, Address, and Maintain, then we have permission to come back to discuss new opportunities.

Security has to be front and center in a Managed Services offering. You want to make security a discipline of your offering, not a specific product. Bundling is key. Once you have a bundle of products, it's no longer a series of commoditized products, but a total security and management package. It's an offing that your competitors will have a hard time matching or competing against. Plus, you can't do a Google search for your Managed Security Services offering, because it is unique to your company. Everyone's program looks a little different. If you brand these programs, you also get the benefit of changing the offering as needs change. Since Choice started offering offsite backup solutions, we have changed the actual underlying product several times to address cost benefits, add new features, and take advantage of technology advancements.

When approaching a prospect for the first time it's important to offer them value for simply engaging with you. Most prospects are reluctant to allow a stranger to come onsite and start making recommendations. As David points out, you have to make it worth their while. We offer a free needs analysis, which is a complimentary basic assessment. Depending on the nature of the sales opportunity, we may invest more or less technician time evaluating the situation. Obviously opportunities that could lead to major recurring revenue as well as larger projects are worth a greater time investment. We want to bring the prospect to the point where we have identified potential points of risk so they can feel that pain. We don't want to give away so much that they can go to a competitor to shop us on price. By asking the correct questions about how the prospect works and what matters to them, we get a sense of whether they are a strong fit for our services, what kind of resources are appropriate to invest in research, and a head start on knowing what products to recommend.

By understanding the market , having a full product mix, and educating prospects, the average reseller company can make the leap from a basic IT support company to a Managed Services company offering Security 2.0.

But it's not simple and it's not cheap. Building the right offering has some challenges. I strongly encourage SMB VARs and other IT services companies to work with companies who have already made the investment and understand this process. This is the time to be selling this type of offering and the right partnership can go a long way in giving you the tools you need to leap over your competition. Even though we have spent a lot of time creating a solid program, it is impossible for one group to do everything needed to cover the entire spectrum of Managed Services. Not only is this a technical challenge, but a management challenge as well. Your clients will not value you because you control lots of different products, but rather because you are guiding them to the solutions they need. In the end they don't really care if it is your product or a hosted white-labeled offering. And once again to reiterate David's point, selling on risk management is a strong pain point to focus on, whether you are selling backups, disaster recovery, system uptime, or anything that would be considered a Managed Service. The key is to get this side of the business up and running quickly to take advantage of a need that is growing and out of control right now.

We offer our security services not only to our clients, but also to resellers who are not able to make the investment in building their own offering. It took us a long time to refine our security offerings and if we knew back then what we know now, we could have saved a lot of time and money. If you happen to be reading this chapter and want to sell these services to your clients, it might make sense to simply rebrand a white label service like the one we provide.

About Choice Technologies, Inc.

Steve Rutkovitz, President of Choice Technologies, and Ben Schmerler, Sales Representative with Choice Technologies have taken the VAR business from traditional break-fix services to managed services, and now to a whole new level with sophisticated security management. Today Choice Technologies, Inc., operates as a full Managed Service Provider (MSP) for Information Technology and Business Process specializing in Security Management. Choice Technologies is one of the leading MSPs of Technology with a complete structured security offering to take organizations from best practices to advance threat detection through their Assess, Address, Maintain model.

To find out more about partnering with Choice Technologies, and how your company might benefit from reselling a managed security program, visit www.choicetechnolgies.com/partners.

CHAPTER TWENTYSIX

The Winning Proposal:

> How to turn the hearts of senior management, high-powered influencers, and other asset owners – Avoiding budgets and competition, and getting away from the point product sale.

The Secret to Selling the Real Solution

The real solution is not a firewall sale. It's much bigger. Any company who simply wants a quote for a new firewall, or firewall upgrade, has thousands or millions of dollars in security work and managed services sitting all around them.

The biggest mistake your sales team can make is to simply quote the firewall. Given the assessment results, vendor-developed security strategies, and your need to close the long-term security opportunity, your goal is to understand the true risk associated with the company you are dealing with. From there you'll formulate a plan, and take your vision to the asset owner.

Remember: Taking your recommendations to the security team at this point, is a waste of time. They can't spend money, have their own biases, and will ask time-wasting questions that confuse the sales process. They don' have any liability and their jobs may be at risk when you discover what a mess their security really is.

By the time you've completed the assessment process using the plan I've outlined in in this book, you should have a strong rapport with the asset owners and other key influencers. Your technical people should have interacted with the client's technical people, and by default his security people. Maintain your executive peer relationship to clarify the buyer's vision of what could be. Think more about the mindsets of the end-users, and their need for greater computing functionality and freedom. Then, figure out how you can make the CISO and CIO, or SMB business owner more successful while addressing their security needs.

In a recent follow-up program, I was asked why attendees consistently hit roadblocks, even when using these principles. I asked for a show of hands on how many people had developed a quality APS. Sadly, no one had. I then asked how many had written, refined, and memorized their value proposition. Several said they wished they had. Finally, I asked them to identify the asset owners. In most cases, they were still dealing with data custodians.

That explains why salespeople were unsuccessful and why a follow-up program is needed. We all need some form of accountability when implementing change, so form an accountability relationship with someone you trust as you execute these concepts. A sales coach is the best choice—someone who will hold your feet to the fire without worrying about offending you. One option is to join my SVLC Insider's Circle Group. Each month I provide insight on topics like these to help sales people make the migration over time. At the end of this book I'll share with you how you can join this program for 30 days, for free.

In addition, I find that people who listen repeatedly to *The Making Money w/ Security and Managed Services* Audio programs (write a book review on Amazon, email me, and I'll send it to you for free), are more confident with their security message. They memorize the phrases and responses to blockers, objections, and concerns. There is a multimillion dollar business on the other side of mastering the security sales process at the asset owner level. But most won't take the time to actually do it.

The Winning Proposal Is Hidden In the Data

Back to the assessment – this is where it starts.

It doesn't matter whether they're performed in India, Australia, Africa, or the United States, they all look fairly similar. The larger integrators tend to have larger clients, so length varies, but even when comparing a report from a large company like Visa to a midsize manufacturer in Chicago, the reports will look similar. The sad part is, none of them are great.

The average assessment conversion rate (the rate at which these documents turn into more projects or managed services) is only about 20%. As I've already stated, consultants, 100% of the time tell me the companies they are assessing are in bad shape. It doesn't make sense that the close rate would be that low. This is clearly a sales problem.

The root problem here comes down to interpreting the data. When I see assessments coming in with executive summaries that read more like vulnerability scans, I know we are in trouble. In a 50 page report, there will be 30 pages of tables generated or reformatted from a scanner. There will be tables and tables of IP addresses with exactly the same unintelligible message about a possible weakness in the network. This is where the SO WHAT? Test comes in. You have to keep asking, "SO WHAT?" until you get to the root of it.

Then at some point the technical consultant will get frustrated and shout out – "SO, PEOPLE CAN GET TO THIS DATA!" Oh! That's what we need to know. Now explain to me how.

The assessment paper won't sell the deal, but it will set the stage for you to sell it in person. The executive deliverable should read more like a briefing, written to that business minded person. It must communicate risk, exposure, and urgency. It can't be filled with IP addresses, model numbers, and Trojan names. All of the data we've alluded to should be thrown into a fat binder labeled "Appendix A", and made available to the IT people after your meeting with the executives. With this document in hand, you're ready to sell it!

Presenting to executives

You're ready to close business! The deal is sold through your presentation, not the assessment document. Always start with the assets. Highly sensitive information and a company's understanding of exposure will sell the next step in the program. Open with a restatement of your value proposition to remind clients of the trends, your concerns, and your differentiation. Tie these to their initiatives and requirements to extend the enterprise. Remember, every strategic decision a company makes today depends on technology, and every technology change calls for a reevaluation of security.

Rather than referring to the network or routers and switches, speak in terms of intellectual capital, customer data, strategic documents, and liability. Stay away from technical topics, which will be addressed in a separate meeting with your technical experts. Focus on the answers given in Question 1: What are you trying to protect?

Relevant Threats

Extending the enterprise brings new risks and exposure. A review of these areas supported by your assessment, will help clients see where they're exposed and where changes are needed. Validate your findings and the company's priorities to reach agreement and a common vision. Business threats include loss of customer confidence, market share, branding and reputation, and competitive advantage—not to mention the liability that comes with losing sensitive data.

Using the house and cloud illustrations, managers can visualize where sensitive data resides and how current computing practices and new company initiatives create greater exposure. This raises awareness of how vulnerable data is.

Company initiatives such as new developments, competitive landscape, political climate, geographic presence, and an upcoming layoff all affect the state of a company's security and relevant threats. This is where your presentation should be focused.

How Comfortable Are You With Your Ability to Detect and Respond?

Keep in mind what the board wants to know. This same format should be used when presenting to any business leader, so here it is once more (memorize this):

- ☐ Top 5-7 threats.
- ☐ What are the odds the company will suffer loss in the next 12 to 18 months?
- ☐ Are they trending up or down?
- ☐ How are they managing to this trend?

Creating the Vision

Begin your remediation plan with the area in which you have the least competition. Bringing up commodity products like antivirus, workstation intrusion protection, firewall, and other tools available at Staples or OfficeMax isn't a good place to start. It's your ability to understand their business and their risks, and to lead them to a safer computing environment that matters. Can you help them become more productive, more competitive, enhance customer experience, and better enable their profit producing end-users, while maintaining a safer date environment? These are the things that enable you to earn your keep.

Highlighting security that can be added to infrastructure products you've previously delivered and implemented is a great place to start. If you've sold this client a network, perhaps it's time to upgrade security controls that can be built in or added to routers and switches. Helping them capitalize on their existing investment and recommending things that are designed for their size company will allow them to see that you understand the economics of their business. SMB companies don't need another sales rep in there trying to sell the Cadillac solution.

Years ago, when Cisco acquired Okena (an intrusion prevention or IPS agent, which eventually became Cisco Security Agent or CSA), resellers were told to lead with this new silver bullet, claiming *Zero Day Protection.* This did not sell like they thought it would! Why? Intrusion prevention software is rapidly becoming a commodity that buyers expect to purchase as part of a suite of security tools. The moment someone brings up IPS Software the buyer thinks of workstation antivirus software ("Don't we already have that in our antivirus software?"). Recovering is almost impossible once you have challenged another decision made by the people in the room.

Change your focus to business enablement, digital assets, security intelligence, and predictive response. Show them ways to achieve enterprise level security controls without disabling the business. They also need ways of leveraging their existing investment, easing management, and providing the capability to work with cloud, BYOD, and collaboration technologies.

Today's mobility and BYOD requirements demand that a company be able to check out users before they connect, and monitor what is happening as they interact with data. A predictive edge is required along with highly sophisticated real-time analysis. Most companies will not be able to afford or staff such a system. Is there a way to deliver this type of security through a hosted solution?

If something malicious is detected, the network must have the intelligence to stop it, quarantine the user, or if required, upgrade or patch the system in question. This approach starts at the network's core, and it will elicit a much different response from the buyer.

The same can be done with storage systems. Rather than looking at the end-node for client protection, start with availability and integrity of data, encryption, or backup-and-restore point objectives. Companies like EMC have been doing this for years, avoiding price wars by selling availability and information management instead of disk space.

Servers can also be sold with security by focusing on availability and business continuity. Again, start where there is no competition, leveraging assets, data location, and the need to build security into the infrastructure.

If you use the cloud diagram, decision makers can connect the last meeting, where they agreed to do the assessment, to the current meeting, where you are putting together the pieces that create a secure computing environment.

You can create a vision by using a series of "What if?" statements.

"What if we could set this up so that when someone with an infected system connects in from home, we know it before they gain access to anything sensitive. In real-time, detection would take place, they would be stopped, perhaps remediated, and then allowed to continue?"

"What if, when someone from your company tried to email account numbers or other sensitive information, our systems detected it and prevented it from happening?"

"What if, when a laptop were stolen, we could track that system, and as soon as it connected to the Internet, anywhere in the world, we would detect it and wipe the disk clean of your company data?"

As you go through these scenarios, addressing issues you've observed or heard in your interviews, you are looking for agreement – people in the room nodding. Now you have concrete recommendations. You know exactly what is going to resonate when you put together your final proposal.

Product Overview

Avoid using acronyms and esoteric technological concepts. Executives won't understand what you're telling them. Instead, relate your diagram to product concepts. Remember: Certain words bring immediate delegation back to IT—a demotion for you. Other words wake up nearby technical people, while losing executives to their iPhone. Don't fall into this trap.

For instance, "Our systems can detect someone trying to connect and analyze their systems, watch their activities, and alert us of any company policy violations." There's no need to go into the details of how NAC or data leakage tools work.

A small appliance may be added internally to create visibility into the client's systems, showing who's accessing what, when they're doing it, and what they're actually doing while connected. This greatly reduces the risks associated with remote access, wireless computing, and perhaps web-server interfaces. It's like setting up parent controls in your home so you know what your kids are up to on the Internet. Simple explanations with simple analogies work best in these meetings. No executive wants to look like an idiot when everyone in the room seems to be nodding to some highly technical description. In most cases no one really knows what is being described, but everyone it too afraid to ask.

The Art of Recommending Next Steps

Don't forget next steps. Every sales call should have a purpose, and the conversion rate depends on your next steps. The next steps are critical. If you don't recommend a road map, either the client will recommend one for you or there won't be one. Your objective is to receive endorsement from the leadership team on the concepts you've described. This will then allow your technical experts to work with the client's technical team on proof of concept projects and actual implementation efforts.

Your technical people should be equipped to bring insights to the IT organization. The company's team may be slow to give up its technology if it competes with yours, especially when brand loyalty has been established through gifts, golf, and free lunches. Gain the sponsorship; then bring in the team.

In my book, *From Vendor to Adviser* I describe in detail how technology consultants on your implementation team should be positioned, allowing you to maintain higher level relationships. This is an essential part of becoming the security advisor to any company.

Evaluations may be required. If so, develop a project plan to manage the process. Don't install free products that people can play with at your expense, even if it's just an opportunity cost. Proof of concept, with preset milestones and agreed-upon next steps, should be your goal.

I Hate Discounts

If your sales process frequently falls into dealing with purchasing officers or discounting services, I recommend studying value pricing methods. Once mastered, they will dramatically improve your personal compensation.

Finally when everything is agreed to—when the vision is established—put it in writing. Take everything you have agreed to and document it. The sale is made in the presentation, not the paper document. In the four meeting model I've briefly referenced, I have personally achieved a 95% close rate on proposals. The details are in the *From Vendor to Adviser* book, but the bottom line is, I only write proposals once I have verbal agreement. This saves an incredible amount of time and stress.

Keep executive documents short and to the point, assume the sale is made in the document, and have a place to sign off. I have provided templates for the proposals I use in my Insider's Circle Forum. Simply visit my website and check out the Insider's Circle Forum under Business Strategy (http://stelzl.us/business-strategy/davids-forums/).

CHAPTER TWENTYSEVEN

The Principles of Winning:

No fail principles of winning more security deals in an overcrowded marketing place – Moving away from point product sales – Working with asset owners – And creating a vision that leads to recurring business

Winning means moving away from product, finding the assets and asset owners, and creating a vision for security within the context of your client's business model. Every company today has a need for more security. And every company that aims to be secure must move away from the "Compliance Mindset" and into a poised stance. They must expect to be compromised at any moment, or perhaps operate with the understanding that there are probably predators in their systems right now. That said, every company needs a team of experts advising them, proactively monitoring their systems and networks, and ready to respond at any moment.

Most companies cannot afford to staff this internally, nor can they afford to purchase and maintain the technology infrastructure to do it themselves. When IT says, "We've got it covered," simply ignore them and continue your ongoing marketing program. Forget about the products, find the asset owners, and begin the process of persuading them to take action.

Don't Take No For An Answer

Most of the time when we think about competition, we respond with the features and benefits that differentiate our company or product. If you're selling a product, you might call in the engineers to argue functionality. If it's a service opportunity, you might be tempted to bring out certifications, resumes, case studies, and perhaps pricing. Your prospects might be asking you to respond to RFPs; other times it's several companies bidding with their own proposals. Often, it comes down to commodity products at the lowest price. Ignore all of this. In most of these cases, you are dealing with people who are acting on a preconceived notion of what they expect to see, and you're talking primarily to people who have no liability – to them, it's just a job.

There are millions of great reasons not to talk to the decision maker. If the average salesperson can come up with one, he will talk himself into using it. You won't win security deals unless you're willing to step out and advise executives.

I do not intend, in this chapter, to compare all of the technologies out there or turn this book into a Sales 101 class. I want to examine some of the strategies used by product manufacturers, look at the strengths and weaknesses of various reseller business models, and bring you back to the foundational principles of justifying security and buying decisions.

If You Really Want to Win

Winning requires a change in strategy. In Napoleon Hill's well know book, *Think and Grow Rich*, he gives us several non-optional steps to take in order to succeed.

Here's a partial list (I highly recommend reading the book):

- ☐ A burning desire.
- ☐ Specialized knowledge.
- ☐ Be a continuous learner.
- ☐ Decisive – not given to fear.
- ☐ Involved in a coaching program.

Inherent in the burning desire is a passion and willingness to work at it. Success doesn't just come because you hope for it, or wish for it. Specialized knowledge requires work. I've given you four key areas to consider, but security is by far the most impactful. If you want this, determine to become THE SECURITY ADVISOR. This is very different from becoming the security technical resource. I am talking about the person who understands business, security trends, business risk, and keeps up with the Wall Street Journal level of what is going on around the world. This is the future of high-performance sales people.

A continuous learner speaks of the person who is studying the trends, reading the security news updates (at the Wall Street Journal Level), and making it part of their weekly discipline to study sales and marketing strategies. At some point every sales person looks the same. Knowing how to really sell and market is the differentiator. Don't be fooled into thinking that sales is natural, or just your title. The continuous learner invests in the books, classes, workshops, seminars, and programs, regardless of your company's expense policies. I am amazed at how many sales managers and company owners expect their sales team to perform without an ongoing sales and marketing development program. If resellers think their vendor partners' training programs are going to do it, they are sadly mistaken. But regardless, the sales person should make the personal investment if they want to be on top and can't get their company to foot the bill.

Fear is disabling. In ten years of coaching just about every sales person I've worked with, many of them top performers, are afraid of senior managers. They are also afraid to become the security expert. Step out and do something different. Study and practice working directly with people in powerful positions. Overcome the fear of failure by doing it. Sure, you will take some falls, but for most, this experience brings with it maturity and eventually success.

Finally, there's mentorship. My father was the one who first pointed this out to me. He started down the road of financial consulting to build his own business. He describes the journey as difficult and tiring. Then one day he met with someone who became his business coach. That person helped him craft his plan, his message, his presentation, and his go-to-market strategy. Using the program they had developed he supported his family well, taking us through private school and college, and making a very comfortable living. Following in his footsteps, when I started this business I immediately sought out coaches to guide me. I have worked with one-on-one coaches, been a member of group coaching programs, and have been involved in mastermind groups over the ten years I've had this business. It's the best investment I've ever made.

Learn From The Deals You've Won

It's always a good idea to review the deals you've won. If you've had the opportunity to win a company over to your way of thinking in the security world, it's helpful to analyze how it happened. We're not talking about making a firewall sale, but convincing a buyer to invest in a more thorough security strategy or to consider security in buying decisions related to infrastructure sales. Perhaps you've sold an in-depth assessment that led to multiple remediation projects. More frequently, I meet people who have sold the assessment, but remediation projects did not follow. It is helpful to understand why.

Over the last year, I've spoken with dozens of salespeople about significant deals they've won. Many were unable to come up with one that represented a total mindset change on the customer's part. Those who could summon an example conveyed a consistent theme: They had a security vision for securing assets—one that involved moving from rank-and-file IT administrators to asset owners. Many leveraged their senior managers or business-savvy security consultants to form a vision for business success. In every case, the process moved the client away from technology and created a safe place to look at applications, assets, and liability.

Case Study

Often, all we can get is an initial meeting with an IT person looking for a quote. I've started there more than once, but the question is, "How can we turn this into a real opportunity?"

A few years ago, I was brought into a deal just like this. As the father of seven children my initial thought was, "This will bring in enough money to enjoy a fast-food dinner at the end of the month." It's not really worth doing. I agreed to attend the meeting on one condition: The buyer must be there. Using a well documented strategy from my book, *From Vendor to Adviser*, I was able to make the move up to their executive management team.

As the meeting opened, I did what I've done many times: I leaned over to my colleague and asked him to put the quote away. This was not a meeting for quotations. I knew that as soon as we pulled out a product quote, the meeting would transition from the buyer to the price and, finally, to the technology, where we'd be stuck for the remainder of the meeting. Once this happens, the decision makers check out, and the big opportunity is lost.

Addressing the economic buyer, I asked the first question: "What are you trying to protect?" As predicted and noted in previous chapters, the dialogue began. The Asset Owner in the room began to talk about applications and data. Sure, the technology people in the room tried to provide some answers, but I kept my focus on applications and data assets, refusing to get into a technical discussion. Facing the Asset Owner, it was difficult for the IT representatives to take charge of the meeting. They tried, but didn't succeed.

After learning about the business, its critical systems, and the importance of certain data maintained, I had a clear understanding of what was really important about this project. I knew the systems, understood the importance of their company's brand, and saw their need to demonstrate security to their customers. From there, we talked about relevant threats and the data owner's comfort level. I learned access control and availability were the primary considerations—not uncommon with many calls I've made. I now had a picture that described the data owner's impact versus likelihood graph—the company's risk model.

Still looking at the data owner, I commented on the firewall's role in providing the kind of security necessary to maintain a safe computing environment. It turned out, as it does in many cases that the firewall was not the major requirement, but merely a supporting element of security at the perimeter. We spent the rest of the meeting talking about business continuity, access control, identity management, and user awareness. The firewall people were bored, but content. I think they may have slept through the remainder of the meeting.

At the end of the meeting, the data owner was convinced we needed to look at these other areas and that some sort of short, high-impact assessment would help us pinpoint where to invest in security. In our recommendations, I verbally pointed out in a private phone call that the firewall he currently had in place was fine, but expensive and not highly available. The final deal included our recommendation on firewall technology, along with identity management, application security, remote connectivity security, and managed services. We ate well at the end of the month.

The lesson here is simple: Ask the question, "What are you trying to protect?" Move the meeting from product to assets, and get the asset owner to talk about what he needs to move his business forward.

Own The Score Card

As you begin working at the project level it is critical that you get involved with the end-users. Our whole industry looks at IT as the influencers, but in many ways they are more like gatekeepers and blockers.

Influencers influence! If you want to see some influential people, look at the people creating and using data to turn a profit. Get in their way and you'll be out of business. When they don't get what they want from IT, they do it themselves with their own budgets. That's why the end-users reported 350 vs. 150 cloud apps in use. They just want to get the job done, and when IT seems too slow, they just do it themselves. The new APP Store world is one where you just go online, find what you need, and do it. They are becoming their own IT.

Last week I had a number of calls with people in my Peak Performers Coaching program. In four meetings, all four new coaching clients admitted they did not have any relationships outside of IT! This is a big mistake.

Somewhere on my blog (www.davidstelzl.us) is a post from the Harvard Business Review explaining that solution selling to the IT department is over – *The Challenger Sale* reaffirms this concept. I go on to talk about how important it is to connect with the people in the company who are moving the company forward. They're not the executives, they're the people who invent stuff, sell the most, manage the biggest clients, etc. These are the people you want to know. Support them in their work and you'll be highly valued.

The guy with the score card is the guy who is measuring improvements. Are you the one enabling this company to move forward? The best possible position you can get into is the one where you hold the score card. When people in the office are asking how something is improving, and others are sending that person to you, you know you have the insider advantage.

CHAPTER TWENTYEIGHT

Product Strategies:

> You can't secure companies without security products. But is your product strategy right for the types of companies you call on, and for the needs your company needs to meet?

Competing Product Strategies

If you're a reseller, you likely sell a number of products that overlap. If you work for a larger manufacturer, you may sell various security products or others that incorporate security. A smaller boutique security company may be focused on security consulting or a point product solution. Each has a distinct strategy and will work to gain buy-in at different organizational levels. It's helpful to consider a variety of strategies to best position your offerings as you identify assets and build justification for investing in security.

The main issue is to avoid competing. As a solution provider, you want to stay away from commodity selling and price wars. The reseller industry is dying for lack of margin.

Vendor Business Models

As I flip through a copy of *SC Magazine,* I see ads from hundreds of security product companies, which can be broken down into three basic types:

Small, niche security product companies, with only one or two products to sell. These companies are often started by entrepreneurs with a technical bent. These individuals once worked for larger companies, had a great idea, and realized their only way to make money was to get out and start a new company. Their goal and strategy are important: At some point, they hope to sell the company to a larger one, similar to the one they left.

Larger security-only companies. Companies like Symantec, SafeNet, Check Point Software, and Websense fall into this category. They believe there's a long-term opportunity in the security market and are buying up technologies to create an end-to-end solution around security. They're securing networks and systems, and in some cases provide managed services around security. Their strategy consists of getting larger clients to buy into the overall data protection strategy they provide.

Corporate giants. Companies like Cisco, Juniper, IBM, and EMC believe security should be built right into their products. If they're building network technology, they don't go to a third party to secure it; they use built-in security and perhaps upgrade to stronger built-in security features. This goes against the second group of manufacturers, but these companies are buying the first group (the small technology companies), and in some cases, the second.

Understanding the Vendor Security Strategy

Many years ago, a company by the name of Network Associates provided clients with a line of products that seemed to have no connection. Network analyzers, helpdesk software, antivirus, encryption and other offerings in a single portfolio gave buyers end-user tools, enterprise management, mid-market call centers, and home user security. In 2004, the company began transforming itself, renaming products under the McAfee brand.

With management changes, the company divested of Magic, Sniffer, and other products that didn't seem to fit. The new company began focusing on security, with acquisitions of Entercept intrusion prevention, Foundstone enterprise scanning, and a number of other technologies, giving McAfee a full suite of security offerings from the desktop anti-x market, network access control (NAC), access control, and managed services. McAfee developed offerings for the enterprise, with clients like Cisco Systems, the mid-market, SMB, and even home users. Its stock went up 40 percent, and execs began to aggressively reengineer their channel. Today this brand has been renamed under their new parent company Intel, as Intel Security Group.

EMC did the same thing when it added RSA and Network Intelligence to its portfolio, along with some others. With the tools to store and back up data, it added security tools for monitoring and access control to drive a stronger security value proposition. EMC went from being a hardware company to a software company, to a business continuity company and finally, a full security company in 2006. In addition, archiving tools for email were added, building on the information life-cycle management message for data security.

BMC Software followed suit after picking up Remedy and Magic (acquired from Network Associates). With the information technology infrastructure library (ITIL) gaining importance and the announcement of ISO 20000, business services management and security merged. Identity management, change control, and the role of the configuration management database (CMDB) in business continuity gave the company a security story and added to

BMC's growing list of "Routes to Value" (a security value proposition).

Finally, there's Cisco. I was sitting in a meeting with thousands of partners back in the mid-'90s, as Cisco announced its three core areas of focus. At that time, the company didn't list security as a focus area, and companies like Check Point Software and ISS (now part of the IBM portfolio) were really heating up. Two years later, Cisco finally announced security as a focus area, and from there began buying up numerous security companies to create a compelling portfolio of security products. While they have gone back and forth on their strategy, recent acquisitions suggest that Cisco sees a strong future in security and has hired me, along with others to retool their sales teams around the world.

The Future is Security – Every Successful Company Sees It

The trends are evident: Security will be part of the infrastructure and part of an overall architectural strategy. Selling point products will result in long, unprofitable sales cycles. In fact, in a recent Forrester Research Paper report, we read about a decline in infrastructure sales in the coming years. Resellers that don't believe this might find their businesses in trouble in the coming years. With this in mind, it's important for resellers to consider the security strategies of the companies for which they resell. Using the assessment tools we have discussed they must begin creating a security vision in the customer's mind, that leverages the entire security solution portfolio provided by a single vendor or group of partnering vendors.

More and more, infrastructure companies are now incorporating baseline security tools right into their products. In addition, many are providing a way to offer a suite of tools through managed cloud based services that can be rebranded by the reseller. This is the vision that should be adopted by the reseller.

CHAPTER TWENTYNINE

Security Reseller Success:

> Just about every reseller claims to offer security. Most just sell security products. Depending on your company focus and team skillset, your approach will change.

Reseller Business Models

Resellers are built on different business models, some stronger than others. In general, the channel is weak in its ability to sell high-end security solutions. This is not to say that strong boutique security companies, large global integrators, or companies coming from the big accounting firms aren't successful. But the percentage of highly skilled security firms is low in the general reseller population or among those who would be classified by manufacturers as major partner resellers.

If you were to look at the number of North American companies that advertise security offerings on their websites and then talk to each one about its actual security project experience, you would find a lack of expertise and real-life project experience. Let's look at some of the models and who's selling security solutions. We can then consider what your firm might look like, or how you can begin building or reengineering your company to achieve greater results.

Climbing The Value Ladder

Before diving into types of resellers, it's helpful to classify your organization on a continuum—from pure product to visionary consulting.

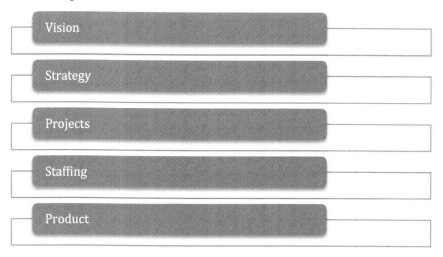

The idea is to get a sense of where in the market your organization is positioned. Is it primarily commodity (product)? In this case, you would fall at the bottom of the diagram above." A visionary company might be like the Chasm Group, made popular by Geoffrey Moore's book *Crossing the Chasm*, which helps companies explore where they're headed, where profitability exists, and how to create direction to get there. This falls right at the top of the stack.

Companies that fall between these two classifications include staff augmentation sold to existing project teams or operational functions. I am talking about things like contracted onsite system administration. Projects would include companies that focus largely on fixed-start and end initiatives, owning the overall scope, development, design, testing, and turnover. Strategy may help companies develop their methodology, process, and workflow. My company would most likely fall between Strategy and Vision, as I work with business owners to develop a company vision, but take them down to a tactical planning process to develop solutions strategies, offerings, and sales-team enablement.

A managed services company would likely be aligned with a project company, but as I explain in the *Making Money w/ Security* Training Program, security should be sold from the assessment, through to the project, and then maintained through a hosted managed solution. All three converge, creating a highly profitable model for the reseller.

If I look primarily at the reseller population, most companies fall somewhere between resource and project. If you are like most, you are working toward more projects, but actually selling more product-install business, which is more like resource business. Low margin, hourly, and commodity in nature. I wrote *From Vendor to Adviser* as a strategy book to help move resellers upstream toward greater profitability. Those who have adopted my recommendations have multiplied their gross profit over time.

Security business is best sold when your company is positioned as a strong project company. Security is then recommended and built into the projects you design and implement. Wherever there's a project initiative with a goal of providing greater functionality, operational efficiency, or enhanced profitability, there is an opportunity to look at risk and remediation on the infrastructure side.

Notice I am not recommending that you remove product from the reseller model, or go completely toward a managed services offering. Instead, become an advisor, get involved early on with project planning, assess security as part of the overall project initiative, remediate and up-fit as required, and recommend an ongoing maintenance strategy where you get paid by the month to oversee it all. Your job becomes one of maintaining an acceptable level of risk as was determined through the assessment process.

In the following subsections, I have taken the classic VAR model and created several subcategories to further define what's successful.

SMB VARs

The smaller VARs, all buying through distribution, generally treat security as a firewall sale. Clients are mostly SMB companies with less than 50 users, with limited buying power. Most of these companies have relegated themselves to break/fix work, network fileserver resale and small networking projects. Over the past ten years just about every one of them has built a managed services offering that is largely based on system monitoring and back up and recovery, which they refer to as "Disaster Recovery." In general, I don't see these companies making great headway in building recurring revenue. Rather there is a fast uptick at the start of their program, and then years of trading back and forth. One client comes on, another leaves for a better price.

Don't be fooled. There is a big security opportunity out there for companies of this size. Your overhead is low (at least it could be), your sales cost is low if you structure your business appropriately, and your sales cycle is short if you sell the right things. Managed services is the place to take this business, and security is the primary driver. When I refer to "security," I mean system availability, data integrity and the ability to restore quickly. SMB companies will never be able to afford the kind of expertise needed to manage all of this apart from a managed services program.

When working with the SMB market, stop focusing on products, and turn everything into a managed offering. Sell the product, but trade the upfront margin for the ongoing contract. The big companies can't afford to take this business, yet it can be very profitable for the company that maintains a small sales force, with low overhead.

Mid-Size VARs

The mid-size reseller has some challenges unique to this market. In general, this group has tried to move upmarket, away from the small companies, and toward companies that actually have IT people. The IT people are generally not well educated in high-tech infrastructure and information security, so there is opportunity; however, IT tends to be territorial in this market.

The security opportunity is growing as hackers recognize a lack of security in the midmarket. Again, it is in the managed services area, but the sale is more difficult. In the SMB market, we had end users without the appropriate support. Influencers are generally willing to create introductions to the decision makers to get the support they need. In this market, you don't have that luxury. Somehow, you have to move up to the decision makers without being delegated downward. Most IT sales are going to be product resale with low margins. Your only hope is to target Asset Owners, convincing them that security is highly specialized and not worth risking with their internal IT group. In most cases, you will be dealing with CFOs or CIOs in name only, who are actually IT director level influencers. Support from other asset owners in the company will be critical in this sales process.

The limiting factor comes in the integrator's willingness to train and invest in higher-end resources with consulting capabilities and business acumen. The need to deal with people on the business side demands a much higher level of expertise as an advisor and consultant.

My recommendation here is to market through executive-only, invitation-only events. I cover this in depth in my *Event Marketing*

Success Tool Kit (available on my store.) The basic idea is to use educational marketing events that appeal to business level people. Using a well planned conversion and follow up process you should be able to convert 50% to 75% or your attendees to the assessment level. Following the guidelines in this book, I would expect companies to drive 80% or 90% of those in the assessment process to project work.

Large Integrators

They might not all be global, but I'm referring to the larger resellers that generally span multiple geographies. These resellers typically sell everything from enterprise storage to data center build-outs, larger network deployments and perhaps applications.

This group generally looks for the bigger opportunities, as overhead is high and the quota requirement demands high-involvement projects. In doing this, a couple of issues arise. First, selling product-install at this level doesn't produce enough profit to create a return on the sale (ROS), unless the accounts are very large and are buying huge quantities of products, making the cost of sale per box low. In other words, there is no net profit once the cost of selling is factored in for the first products sold. As a result, many salespeople steer away from security sales, thinking of security as a firewall with little margin.

Another issue is the larger companies' unwillingness to hire specialized security consultants. Great security consultants often demand higher pay than in other niche areas. As a result, corporate managers skimp on security skills, favoring generalists in the networking group to carry out specialized assignments like security assessment work. The result should be apparent: The assessment becomes a list of network vulnerabilities routed straight to the network administrator's desk. Remediation projects never materialize, and people wonder why security is hard to sell. If you look at the average large integrator, who is not a security specialty integrator, their security history will be scattered. They will likely have a historical path of hiring one security leader, that person leaving within two years, and a new one emerging. The trend probably dates back over the past fifteen years.

The solution: Hire people with consulting skills, security experience, and an interest in the bigger security picture. Focus on business continuity, security assessments, and risk analysis. Then move things toward a security managed services offering with reoccurring revenue potential.

Security Boutiques

I am convinced many security boutiques exist because of the issues raised in the last section—primarily pay. I can think of at least five companies started by people who once worked for me, under the umbrella of a larger company. The larger company was unwilling to meet their salary requirements, so they left to form new companies focused solely on security. To my knowledge, they are all profitable and growing their bottom line. In addition, I have coached many entrepreneurial teams as they ramp up new security-oriented companies. I expect them to succeed.

These companies are doing well because there's a market for consultants who understand the value of assets, the risks associated with the Internet, and the need companies have to adopt new, less secure applications of technology such as BYOD. Boutiques are good at demonstrating value and showing their clients how to defend against today's cyber-criminals, and they are valued for their deep technical expertise. In every case, this is a recipe for success.

Resellers can duplicate this within their existing business structure if they take the appropriate steps. Most of the puzzle is solved by getting the right people and empowering them.

Managed Services Companies

This last category of companies is largely comprised of resellers who primarily offer managed services. They are, in fact, security companies, however most don't apply a risk-based sales model. If they did, they would be more successful. Managed Services is almost always a risk mitigation decision.

What I mean is this; when a company invests in a managed services offering, it is almost always to avoid some kind of risk. That might be disaster recovery or back up management, or it might be having someone oversee the systems administration function to ensure performance. Whatever the reason, they are trying to maintain system availability, data integrity, or data privacy. These are the three pillars of security.

Resellers have bought into the idea that managed services offer a new opportunity for margin as products commoditize; however, many of these companies are not succeeding. Why? Because they don't understand the risk-based sales model. There is little value in monitoring just for the sake of monitoring. Decision makers are looking for risk reduction. Somehow, these companies must measure need and then demonstrate a reduction in risk. This is an impact vs. likelihood sale. When managed services are justified on something other than risk, price comparisons often creep in over time, causing that company to lose the contract to another low-priced provider.

CHAPTER THIRTY

The Foundation of a Winning Security Provider

Principles of winning, regardless of whether your company builds product or resells technology.

Regardless of whether you're a solution provider reseller or a manufacturer, there are certain principles that make a winning approach.

Focus on Assets, Not Products. Asset-level conversations directly address the needs of the buyer. Anything else gets delegated to non-decision makers, creating an endless sales cycle.

Silo Versus Integrated. Treating security as one of your offerings makes it a product sale. An asset sale must be integrated into another solution that addresses a business need. This is where assets are created and used, and where liability and justification are found.

Request Response vs. Need Creation: Responding to RFPs means you are responding to a security sale that was actually made by someone else. It's now down to a price decision. To win, you must change the rules, expose risks, create a vision for what could be done, and seize the opportunity to advise asset owners—a job worth paying for. I've written this book to avoid the commodity/price sale - to teach sales people how to discover the security opportunities before an IT organization is out price shopping.

Buy and Sell vs. Sell and Build. Companies that buy or make products are selling the commodity. The company that creates the vision and customizes security according to the impact vs. likelihood graph is the one worth hiring.

Engineers vs. Security Specialists. Even though a silo approach is discouraged, you still need experts to understand the risk. This is where boutique security companies have won large accounts without having the enormous sales presence of a global integrator. Specialization creates the foundation for the advisor.

The Secret to Finding New Business w/ Security

Once you have a message that works, it's time to start contacting people. Who will you call? The tendency is to take leads from the manufacturer. When you get a lead, your first reaction is to discover product needs. This is pure commodity business. Once a buyer knows what he needs and begins the process of procurement, price has become the differentiator. 80% of the products being purchased today were researched on Google long before they called you.

Focus on the group that doesn't understand threats. Identify data owners within the accounts you call on, and begin developing your impact vs. likelihood story. Use your value statements to get their attention, and be prepared with a compelling value proposition. Begin the process of educating IT leaders and asset owners on the business side. Begin building a vision with people who have liability and are directly affected when compromises occur.

The Two-Year Marketing Plan

Do these principles guarantee a win? Nothing is a sure thing. We're dealing with people, not machines. It's impossible to predict what people will do. Many factors influence how managers and executives respond to your message. This doesn't mean you should throw everything away.

People need a vision. Start with a strong APS (Advisor Positioning Statement), and begin collecting the information you need to remain in contact with them. Use your contact database to group similar prospects or clients—those who may be interested in the same information. Then, start collecting information as you read, interact with others, and learn about new industry trends.

Think of yourself as a coach, providing information that will help people make better business decisions. Rather than pestering them with weekly phone calls, asking them if they're ready to buy something, begin providing value to them. Don't overwhelm them with spam. Use a timely, methodical approach to send them targeted information. I call these efforts "idea emails." Here's an example:

Hi, John:

Over the last few months, I have been working with a few companies similar to yours on migrating to the Cloud. Given recent trends in data theft, I want to share some ideas I have with you. I would like to set up a short call—perhaps next Tuesday or Thursday, if this works for you. Please let me know if you have a few minutes, and I'll give you a call.

Next, I send hundreds of these emails, hoping only a few people will respond. With a database of about 4,500 contacts, I send notes to people who fall into all of my defined groups. It takes time to build this database, but with the APS it doesn't take long. Every week, someone emails me in response. I have basically eliminated cold-calling through this process.

Follow these guidelines for email success:

- Short message.
- Personal email format.
- No acronyms or tech talk.
- Not written in HTML (like a marketing letter).
- Casual and personal.
- Addressed to an individual—not a group—so it appears to be the only email I've sent.
- Aimed at raising curiosity about a specific topic that's relevant to my prospect.
- Proposes two time slots to hundreds of people; not left open-ended.
- Doesn't beg for the meeting; sounds confident.
- Foreshadows that you have something to say when the meeting occurs.

I use Infusionsoft to create a customized email campaign that's addressed to individuals, and I contact them monthly with a sequence of three email. My messages don't show up as spam, nor am I giving away the email addresses of others I'm contacting.

Combine this with events using industry experts on relevant security topics, which target asset owners.

Over time, if you are providing valuable information. People will keep you in mind when issues come up. New applications, business expansion, and strategy meetings will become opportunities. As people respond to my emails each week, they frequently apologize for ignoring the many messages I've sent over the months, indicating the last one hit them and they're ready to talk. If this happens weekly, your cold-calling efforts will become unnecessary.

Start today with your APS, and begin collecting as many contacts as you can in a given quarter. Track how these relationships progress. Is your APS effective? Did you connect with this person? Is there an opportunity to stay in contact with relevant information? If so, you are bound to have success in using the principles in this book to drive your security business. Remember: Security is not a product; it's a discipline. Use it to attract people who make decisions and have liability. Upon positioning yourself as a trusted advisor, sell them the products and services your company is developing to meet the needs of today's businesses.

For an in-depth discussion on marketing best practices, first review the value proposition concepts in my book, *From Vendor to Advisor*, then work through the *Event Marketing Success Kit* Concepts. Finally, consider other resources such as Seth Godin's book, *Permission Marketing*. **Sales people who master marketing will always outsell the sales person with deep product knowledge.**

Resources To Get You Started

Now, if you really want to make this work, there are tools and resources, videos, and more to help you. Following I have included several opportunities, including a free website with great ideas, tools, and updates to the information presented here!

JOIN the House & Cloud Private Site….this is **free** to anyone who has this book. So that's you. On my private site you'll find videos, resources, and updates, as well as a place to collaborate and ask questions! Follow this link to gain access!

http://security.stelzl.us/hcmembers

Master The Security Sale!

If you really want to master the security sale, you can do it right now. Join the Security Sales Mastery Program^{SM}. You can read more about it and sign up right here:

http://stelzl.us/business-strategy/mastery-programs/sell-security/

This sales training is much more than "Training". It's an intensive training/coaching program. You'll master the message I use to attract CIO and Business Owner buyers – anyone fitting the "Asset Owner" profile. You'll discover how to create a powerful message to move them forward. If you want to grow your business, this is the fastest way to do it.

Then, as you go along you will have access to collaborate directly with me – exchanging ideas and working around the hurdles that slow down your sales progress.

You'll also have access to many more of the resources on my growing private membership site. Videos, audios, templates, and more.

Don't wait – join hundreds of other sales and marketing professionals who are using this material to fill their pipelines and bring business to a close.

FREE – Special Report on Converting Prospects into Customers!

http://morecustomers.stelzl.us/specialreport

ABOUT DAVID STELZL

David Stelzl brings a fresh perspective on the high-tech consulting business. He's taken resellers from simply selling products, to providing high-end technology programs, significantly increased company profits, and has had the privilege of training many sales and marketing organizations worldwide on how to reach executive managers with a compelling security value proposition.

He has authored several books including the first edition of *The House & the Cloud*, *Data@Risk*, and *From Vendor to Adviser*. Each year David addresses audiences around the world in both online and live events. His experience and insights continue to bring new perspective on how the reseller model should work, how high-tech solutions should be positioned, and how to maintain margins in a commoditizing industry of networks and computers.

His firm, Stelzl Visionary Learning Concepts, Inc. has consulted with, addressed, or been sponsored by clients such as Cisco Systems, Hewlett Packard, Ingram Micro, Trend Micro, Symantec, Check Point, Juniper, Kaspersky, and many solution providers including Accuvant, ePlus, Presidio, CDW, and Verizon Business.

David earned his CISSP certification in 2000, and has worked in the information security market since 1995.

15861072R00152

Printed in Great Britain
by Amazon